Peace Operations

SECOND EDITION

PAUL F. DIEHL AND
ALEXANDRU BALAS

polity

First edition published in 2008 by Polity Press

This edition published in 2014 by Polity Press

Polity Press
65 Bridge Street
Cambridge CB2 1UR, UK

Polity Press
350 Main Street
Malden, MA 02148, USA

ISBN-13: 978-0-7456-7180-2
ISBN-13: 978-0-7456-7181-9 (pb)

A catalogue record for this book is available from the British Library.

Typeset in 10.25 on 13 pt Scala by
Servis Filmsetting Ltd, Stockport, Cheshire
Printed and bound in Great Britain by Clays Ltd, St Ives plc

The publisher has used its best endeavours to ensure that the URLs for external websites referred to in this book are correct and active at the time of going to press. However, the publisher has no responsibility for the websites and can make no guarantee that a site will remain live or that the content is or will remain appropriate.

For further information on Polity, visit our website: www.politybooks.com

Peace Operations

War and Conflict in the Modern World Series

L. Brock, H. Holm, G. Sørensen and M. Stohl, *Fragile States*
Feargal Cochrane, *Ending Wars*
Matthew Evangelista, *Law, Ethics and the War Terror*
J. Michael Greig and Paul F. Diehl, *International Mediation*
Janie Leatherman, *Sexual Violence and Armed Conflict*
Andrew Mumford, *Proxy Warfare*
Dennis Sandole, *Peacebuilding*
Eric Shibuya, *Demobilizing Irregular Forces*
Timothy Sisk, *Statebuilding*
Rachel Stohl and Suzette Grillot, *The International Arms Trade*
Paul Viotti, *American Foreign Policy*
Thomas G. Weiss, *Humanitarian Intervention*

Contents

List of Figures and Tables

CHAPTER ONE

Introduction

Throughout most of the history of the modern state system (post 1648), and even before, the primary mechanisms to deal with violent conflict were limited. Diplomacy was always an option, albeit underutilized, and negotiated agreements between states occurred. Too often, however, diplomacy was more effective in ending a war than in preventing one. More commonly, coercive instruments were the primary mechanisms used by states to deal with threats to peace and security. Strategies based on deterrence, alliance formation, and the direct use of military force were how individual states sought to preserve their security and promote their interests.

In the twentieth century, diplomacy and coercion remained the most prominent tools for foreign policy decision-makers, but the rise of international organizations expanded the range and form of options. Among the most notable was the development of peacekeeping, a novel use of soldiers in non-traditional roles coordinated most often by international organizations rather than national governments. Peacekeeping has gradually evolved to encompass a broad range of different conflict management missions and techniques, which are incorporated under the term "peace operations."[1]

This book provides an overview of the central issues surrounding the development, operation, and effectiveness of peace operations. How did peace operations evolve out of more coercive uses of military forces? When did traditional peacekeeping missions give way to more expansive peace operations? Chapter 2 provides a historical narrative on peace operations, beginning in earlier centuries and, most importantly, noting the dramatic changes in conflict management with the creation of the League of Nations. The chapter also provides an overview of early peace operations – traditional peacekeeping during the Cold War and the panoply of missions since the early 1990s. Patterns across time and space are noted and explained. Peace operations are not deployed to all conflicts in the world. Accordingly, the latter part of this chapter summarizes the empirical findings on the conditions for when and where peace operations are deployed, as well as the factors that affect how long they last.

Who organizes peace operations, and how are they managed? Peace operations are now organized by different agencies and with a variety of operational arrangements. Chapter 3 describes the different kinds of organizational schemes. The discussion includes an analysis of the relative advantages and disadvantages of having a peace operation organized by the United Nations (UN), regional organizations, multinational groupings, and other institutional arrangements. Peace operations are generally organized on an ad hoc basis, and the process for supplying personnel and funding the operations is also discussed. Few analysts would argue that such arrangements are optimal, but political and other constraints necessitate this system. Special attention is given to so-called multiple simultaneous peace operations, or MSPOs, in which more than one agent is involved in a given peace operation or set of operations (Balas 2011a). The chapter also provides a description and assessment of various alternatives to the present methods of organization and financing.

What does it mean for peace operations to be successful, and what conditions are associated with such success? Chapter 4 discusses different criteria and operational indicators according to different stakeholders in the conflict – the disputants, the local population, the organizing agency, and the international community. The bulk of the chapter is devoted to summarizing research on peace operation effectiveness, dividing the causal factors into operational (e.g., mandate), contextual (e.g., civil vs. interstate conflict), and behavioral (e.g., behavior of third parties) influences.

What is the future of peace operations? They have evolved over the last almost seventy years in large part as a result of changing conflict conditions and as decision-makers have learned from past mistakes. The concluding chapter looks at the emerging conflict trends and identifies ten challenges for peace operations in the twenty-first century, with special attention to their implications and the possible policy choices to address them.

Before addressing these questions, it is necessary to define the scope of this study. The term "peace operations" may seem obvious, and most people will have the shared image of a blue-helmeted soldier in mind when they hear the term. Yet peace operations encompass a variety of different phenomena, and such distinctions may be critical for the kind of policy choices that the international community must make.

Concepts

Discussions of peace operations are notorious for their conceptual muddles. It is common for the terms "peacekeeping," "peacebuilding," "peace enforcement," "peacemaking," and a host of other terms to be used interchangeably. NATO's Supreme Allied Commander in Europe, General John Craddock, expressed it well: "Peacekeeping is a very ambiguous term."[2] Indeed, the United Nations labels a broad set of operations over time as "peacekeeping," implying similar attributes when in fact there are dramatic differences among the operations covered under this umbrella.

Elucidating the conceptual distinctions between different kinds of peace operations is essential for understanding how these have changed over time, and ultimately for the practical limits to the success of those operations. A good starting point is using what might be called "traditional" peacekeeping (also referred to as "Cold War" peacekeeping) as a baseline category; most other forms of peace operations developed from this original conception. In defining traditional peacekeeping operations, a comparison with standard military operations is enlightening for indicating not only what traditional peacekeeping is, but also what it is not.

Traditional Peacekeeping
Traditional peacekeeping forces are deployed to a war-torn area in order to achieve several purposes. Most notably, they seek to limit the violent conflict that occurs in the area. The primary mechanism for this is the deployment of troops as an interposition or buffer force that separates the combatants following a ceasefire. These troops are multinational, coming usually from at least a dozen or more countries, and generally deploy under the leadership of the United Nations. As noted below, the size, rules of engagement, and military capacity of a peacekeeping force are insufficient to stop a determined party from attacking its opponent; Israeli forces quickly broke through peacekeeping lines (UNIFIL) in southern Lebanon during the 1982 invasion. How, then, do peacekeeping forces promote peace? By separating combatants at a physical distance, peacekeepers prevent the accidental engagement of opposing armies, thereby inhibiting small incidents that could escalate to renewed war. They also prevent deliberate cheating on ceasefire agreements, as violations can be more easily detected. The physical separation of the protagonists provides early warning of any attack and thereby decreases the tactical advantages that stem from a surprise attack. Renewed warfare

in which the aggressor can be identified by the peacekeepers and in which peacekeepers are partly the target of that aggression is also likely to produce international condemnation. The costs in international reputation and possible sanctions, combined with the decreased likelihood of quick success, are designed to be sufficient to deter any attack (Fortna 2008).

Traditional peacekeeping is also predicated, at least in part, on promoting an environment suitable for conflict resolution. Peacekeepers do not engage in diplomatic initiatives themselves, although other personnel from the sponsoring organizations (e.g., the UN) may do so. Rather, they are thought to create the conditions conducive to the hostile parties resolving their differences (a claim that is evaluated in chapter 4). There are several rationales why intense conflict is deleterious to mediation and negotiation, and why a ceasefire promotes the conditions under which mediators can facilitate an agreement between the opposing sides. First, a cooling-off period, evidenced by a ceasefire, can lessen hostilities and build some trust between the protagonists. In times of armed conflict, leaders and domestic audiences become both habituated and psychologically committed to the conflict, and some segments of the population profit politically and economically from the fighting. Before diplomatic efforts can be successful, this process must be broken or interrupted, something in which peacekeepers can assist by maintaining a ceasefire.

Second, intense conflict puts domestic political constraints on leaders who might otherwise be inclined to sign a peace agreement. Negotiating with the enemy may have significant political costs during active hostilities. Calls for ceasefires or pauses in bombing attacks in order to promote negotiations and diplomatic efforts are consistent with this underlying logic. Of course, this presumes that hostilities harden bargaining positions and attitudes rather than leading to concessions by parties suffering significant costs. Third,

Table 1.1 Traditional peacekeeping vs. military operations		
Dimension	Traditional peacekeeping	Military operations
Host state consent	Yes	No
Impartiality	Yes	No
Use of force	Self-defense	Offensive
Size	Small	Very large
Equipment	Lightly armed	Heavily armed

and from a somewhat different vantage point, active conflict leads decision-makers to concentrate on those ongoing hostilities (a short-term concern), and therefore they will not place settlement issues (a longer-term concern) high on their agendas. That is, during heightened armed conflict, political and diplomatic attention will be devoted to the conduct of the fighting and, at best, to immediate conflict management issues such as securing a ceasefire. Fourth, that peacekeepers have been provided may signal to the disputants the willingness of the international community to commit additional resources to any settlement that would follow their deployment.

Differences with Military Operations   As is evident from the strategy of traditional peacekeeping, such operations are significantly different from military ones. Yet peacekeeping and military missions differ on a number of other dimensions as well, as summarized in table 1.1.

Traditional peacekeeping operations are based on the so-called holy trinity: host-state consent, impartiality, and minimum use of force (Bellamy, Williams, and Griffin 2010). The first requirement is that peacekeeping forces must have the permission of the state on whose territory they will be deployed. Such permission can also be withdrawn, and peacekeepers must leave accordingly, as was the case with

UN troops in the Sinai (UNEF I) just before the 1967 Arab–Israeli War when Egypt withdrew its permission. The idea that military forces in war would need the permission of the state against which they are fighting is, of course, absurd. Yet traditional peacekeeping forces rely on host-state consent, just as they rely on the cooperation of the combatants to maintain peace.

The second component, impartiality, indicates that the peacekeepers are not intended to favor one combatant over another; there is no designated aggressor, and the peacekeeping forces are to implement their mandate without discrimination. In contrast, military interventions are usually biased, as soldiers and equipment are sent to alter the balance of power in the conflict by supporting one actor against another. The third leg of the trinity, minimum use of force, refers to the rules of engagement permitted to peacekeeping soldiers. Peacekeepers are usually constrained to use military force only in self-defense. In contrast, military forces regularly employ offensive military tactics, and the level of force is theoretically constrained only by necessity and the rules of international humanitarian law.

Traditional peacekeeping operations are also noticeably different in their appearance from military ones. Peacekeeping forces are relatively small, with an average of fewer than 10,000 troops during the Cold War era. Military actions, such as the 500,000 troops in the first Persian Gulf War and the 150,000 American troops during the occupation of Iraq, are much larger. Consistent with differences in size, purpose, and rules of engagement, traditional peacekeeping units are lightly armed, typically with only rifles or side arms. Military units, especially those of the major powers, are equipped with advanced technology, including armored vehicles, missiles, and precision guided weapons.

For the Cold War period, the overwhelming majority of

operations fitted the profile of traditional peacekeeping (see the development of peace operations in chapter 2). An example is the United Nations Peacekeeping Force in Cyprus (UNFICYP), in place since 1964. This changed with the end of the Cold War in the late 1980s and the proliferation of new peace operations. With this, host-state consent, impartiality, and the use of force became less defining features than variables along continuums. So too did the terminology change, as what was covered under peacekeeping became quite expansive. Most prominent in the post-Cold War era has been peacebuilding.

Peacebuilding
There is not necessarily agreement among scholars and practitioners on the conceptual components of peacebuilding, and therefore it is impossible to specify a single, universally agreed upon definition. Nevertheless, there is some intersubjective consensus on some of the relevant dimensions of peacebuilding operations. A useful place to begin is the definition put forward by then UN Secretary-General Boutros Boutros-Ghali (1995),[3] the baseline conceptualization of all peacekeeping-related definitions used by scholars and policymakers.[4] Boutros-Ghali speaks of "peacebuilding" as the "creation of a new environment," not merely the cessation of hostilities facilitated by traditional peacekeeping. His analysis and the analyses of other scholars seem to suggest a series of characteristics or dimensions by which peacebuilding can be compared with other concepts.

The first dimension concerns the goal(s) of peacebuilding. There is general agreement that, minimally, the purpose of peacebuilding is to prevent the recurrence of conflict. Yet there is some disagreement over whether this idea of "negative peace" (the absence of violent conflict) should be extended to encompass elements of "positive peace," including reconciliation, value transformation, and justice concerns. This distinction is critical, because virtually all differences in conceptualizations of peacebuilding can be traced back to disagreements on this point.

The second dimension of peacebuilding involves the strategies and accompanying activities designed to achieve the goal(s). Not surprisingly, these vary somewhat according to whether or not one pursues goals broader than preventing conflict recurrence. A minimalist strategy of preventing conflict recurrence adopts strategies consistent with conflict management. That is, peacebuilding is concerned partly with decreasing the opportunity to resort to violence, consistent with the purposes of traditional peacekeeping. Yet, some peacebuilding activities go beyond traditional peacekeeping, including disarming warring parties, destroying weapons, and training indigenous security personnel. Some peacebuilding conceptions are also dedicated to creating mechanisms whereby conflicts can be managed peacefully rather than through violence. Thus, facilitating elections, repatriating refugees, and strengthening government institutions are peacebuilding activities consistent with this strategy.

A broader conception of peacebuilding leads to somewhat different strategies and sets of activities. Some see peacebuilding as addressing the "root causes of conflict." Minimalist conceptions expect conflict to occur but desire to manage it peacefully. In contrast, the maximalist strategy promotes not merely management but conflict resolution – that is, eliminating the "willingness" of parties to use violence. Accordingly, many peacebuilding activities are designed for attitudinal changes by disputants and their constituents. These include programs to promote economic development and human rights protection.

A third dimension concerns the timing of such activities. Most conceptions of peacebuilding envision its activities to occur following some type of peace settlement between warring parties. This is in contrast to other forms of conflict management. Preventive diplomacy and its accompanying actions are supposed to be put in place before significant levels of violence occur. Coercive military intervention takes place in the context of ongoing armed conflict. Traditional peacekeepers (e.g., the UNDOF force in the Golan Heights) are usually deployed after the cessation of violence but before any peace settlement (hence their primary roles as ceasefire monitors). Peacebuilding then takes places after prevention failed, after traditional peacekeeping (if it occurred), and after peacemaking (see discussion below on conflict phases).

There is an implicit assumption in peacebuilding that the existence of a prior war has fundamentally changed the relationship (and relative risk of future conflict) such that the strategies and activities pursued must be different; diplomatic initiatives alone are likely to be inadequate. Positive peace advocates note that there is no reason to confine peacebuilding activities to post-settlement, as many could be employed with positive results in earlier phases of conflict as well. They are certainly correct in this assertion, and indeed instances of such (e.g., KFOR actions in Kosovo) have occurred, but, in practice, peacebuilding conducted by international governmental organizations, is predominantly a post-war set of actions.

A fourth dimension is the context in which peacebuilding should be carried out. Boutros-Ghali (1995) envisions that it could occur following either interstate or intrastate conflict. *De facto*, however, most of the discussion of peacebuilding has assumed that it would be employed in a civil context, following an intrastate war or significant ethnic conflict, or even in a failed state. In practice, we should recognize that the distinctions between intrastate and interstate conflict break down when neighboring states intervene in civil conflicts, best illustrated by the Congo war starting in the 1990s.

The fifth and final dimension concerns the actors who will carry out the peacebuilding actions. As Pugh (2000) notes, peacebuilding seems to assume that external actors will play a significant, if not an exclusive, role in this enterprise. Again, an examination of the strategy and activities would not seem to preclude local actors, and indeed some elements (e.g., truth and reconciliation commissions) may be more successful when external actors are not the driving force. Also implicit in the peacebuilding notion is that such actors will act in an impartial fashion for the greater good of the society, exercising some moral authority rather than pursuing private interests. Normatively, most regard peacebuilding as an altruistic enterprise, but, as Pugh argues, such conceptions may still promote particular ideologies (e.g., democracy, neo-capitalism, and the like).[5] Peacebuilding operations are confined largely to the post-Cold War era, and indeed most peace operations then have at least some peacebuilding components. Examples are the UN Operation in Burundi (ONUB), the UN Transitional Administration in East Timor (UNTAET), and the UN Integrated Peacebuilding Office in Guinea-Bissau (UNIOGBIS).

Other Related Terms
In the course of studying peace operations, analysts are likely to come across other terms that may or may not be used in conjunction with such operations. For clarification purposes, several are worth noting. The terms "new peacekeeping" and "second-generation" peacekeeping generally refer to the first wave of post-Cold War peacekeeping operations that adopted certain missions beyond those associated with traditional peacekeeping (e.g., election supervision), including some now associated with peacebuilding (e.g., humanitarian assistance). "Robust" peacekeeping (also referred to as "muscular" peacekeeping) is often used to describe recent peace operations that

involve more permissive rules of engagement, including the offensive use of military force to establish order.

At first glance, "peace enforcement" may appear to be an oxymoron, but generally it refers to missions in which soldiers undertake coercive missions (e.g., stopping armed hostilities). Peace enforcement differs from robust peacekeeping largely in degree, in that the former has greater military capacity and a mandate to prevent the renewal of warfare and to punish those responsible for such hostilities, and is thereby closer to a conventional military operation. Many of the terms that relate to specific peace operation missions are discussed more fully in the next section. Two other terms that appear in Boutros-Ghali's book (1995) and that are part of the peace operation lexicon are "preventive diplomacy" and "peacemaking," respectively. The former refers to a variety of efforts designed to prevent disputes from arising between actors or to deter their spread once they do occur. Peace operations may play a preventive role, but preventive diplomacy may more likely involve sending special representatives or negotiation teams to a region rather than deploying troops. Similarly, peacemaking involves a range of actions designed to promote a peace agreement or conflict resolution between hostile parties. Peace operations are not generally charged with that responsibility directly, and Boutros-Ghali specifically identifies other diplomatic and legal techniques to achieve this, including mediation and resort to international courts. As noted above, however, traditional peacekeeping is designed to influence the environment under which peacemaking occurs, even if it cannot impose conflict resolution directly. Finally, other, newer terms referring to specific types of peacekeeping activities (humanitarian intervention, human security, and responsibility to protect) are discussed in chapter 2.

Classifying Different Missions

During the Cold War era, peacekeeping missions could be classified largely by the political context of the disputes with which they dealt. Using a broad conception of peacekeeping and reviewing all operations before 1990, James (1990) classified these in four categories according to the relationship of the conflict to surrounding states. "Backyard Problems" were those that take place within the sphere of a major power. "Clubhouse Troubles" occur when a group of states organize an operation to deal with an "in-group" problem. "Neighbourhood Quarrels" are those conflicts that do not fall into the first two categories, remain largely localized, but do not reach the level of "Dangerous Crossroads," which are those conflicts most prone to escalation and the greater involvement of external parties.

Nevertheless, they all roughly shared the same mandate or mission. Such operations were dedicated to being interposition forces (i.e., separating combatants) which performed ceasefire monitoring functions. Some peace observation missions were too small in number and were unarmed, and therefore did not necessarily function as a buffer between the disputants. Nevertheless, the passive monitoring of a temporary peace agreement was the hallmark of traditional operations.

One of the greatest changes in peace operations over the past decade has been the dramatic expansion in the number and types of tasks they might now be asked to perform. Yet, it is not always clear how different these new missions really are and what implications there might be for the success, and the factors affecting that success, of the mission.

Bellamy, Williams, and Griffin (2010) place operations within seven categories based largely on the broad goals of the operation. "Preventive Deployments" are designed to operate in the first phase of conflict (see below) in contexts in which there is a significant risk of armed conflict, but widespread violence has not yet occurred. Preventive peacekeeping operations are designed to forestall the outbreak of violence or prevent its spread from proximate states or areas in which it has already occurred. The United Nations Preventive Deployment Force (UNPREDEP) in Macedonia was put in place toward the end of the Bosnian civil war in order to stabilize this neighboring area. "Traditional Peacekeeping" is as described above, and the first UN Emergency Force (UNEF I) operation deployed to the Sinai in 1956 is the classic example.

"Wider Peacekeeping" occurs with the consent of the disputants, as does traditional peacekeeping, but there are a number of deviations from that conventional model. Wider operations occur during ongoing violence (primarily intrastate), involve broader and often changing sets of tasks (e.g., humanitarian aid, protecting civilians), and require greater coordination with non-governmental organizations (NGOs). The United Nations Protection Force (UNPROFOR) in Bosnia is cited as an example. "Peace Enforcement" refers to missions that are designed to be proactive and authorized under Chapter VII of the UN Charter. These resemble collective or multilateral security operations (e.g., UN actions during the Korean War), with significant use of military coercion to restore peace and redress aggression. Some might argue that such missions do not fall under the peace operation rubric, but Bellamy and his colleagues cite the first United Nations Operation in Somalia (UNOSOM I) as having elements of this kind of operation.

"Assisting Transitions" includes cases in which peace operations help facilitate the change from war to peace, and these are usually carried out in the context of a peace settlement agreement. They rely on the same three components (consent, impartiality, and minimum use of force) as traditional peacekeeping but involve more complex tasks such as election supervision. The UN Transitional Authority in Cambodia, or UNTAC (1992–3), which helped conduct democratic elections after the end of an internationalized civil war, is an example. Similar functions are carried out by "Transitional Administrations," but there are a number of notable differences. In contrast to assistance missions, these operations involve the temporary assumption of sovereign authority and government functions, as well as the imposition of peace through military force with robust rules of engagement; these administration missions therefore do not follow the aforementioned "holy trinity" principles. Thus far, such operations have been confined to small geographic areas, as evidenced by the UN Transitional Administration in East Timor (UNTAET).

Finally, "Peace Support Operations" are multidimensional missions with a substantial civilian component. In many ways, these are what have been referred to as peacebuilding operations, with greater emphasis on the use of necessary force and a variety of different mission tasks. NATO's Implementation Force (IFOR) operation in Bosnia, starting in 1995, is listed as an example.

Even accepting such categories does not mean that operations are homogeneous, and indeed some operations mutate over their lifetimes, taking on several different missions. For example, Talentino (2004) divides peacebuilding operations into three categories: limited, extensive, and nation-building. She seems to make such distinctions based on the operation's enforcement powers, scope of reform activities, timing of deployment, and degree of control over the local government machinery. Empirically, peacebuilding operations vary substantially by mandates and functions according to the kinds of conflicts with which they are asked to deal and the specific contextual needs where they are deployed.

How similar or different are the missions performed within

these categories? Diehl, Druckman, and Wall (1998) sought to measure the degrees of difference between missions. They examined twelve different peace missions across twelve different dimensions suggested by the scholarly literature and peacekeeping experts; among such dimensions were the level of control over the conflict, the ease of mission exit, and the clarity of goals.

The way in which the missions are grouped or clustered in the space indicates similarities that serve to reduce the twelve missions to fewer, more general types. Using traditional peacekeeping as a point of reference, four other distinct groupings are apparent. Election supervision, arms control verification, and observation are grouped together; these missions have in common a monitoring function and are relatively passive. Two missions are intended to limit damage to conflicting societies: humanitarian assistance and preventive deployment. Four missions have the function of restoring countries to functioning civil societies: protective services, intervention in support of democracy, pacification, and state-/nation-building. Two missions distant from traditional peacekeeping are combat-oriented coercive (or offensive) missions: sanctions enforcement and collective enforcement.

Placing missions in different groups is not merely a classificatory exercise. There are implications for how we analyze, evaluate, and train for peace operations. First, we know that many peace operations undertake multiple missions either simultaneously or sequentially. For example, UNPROFOR in Bosnia had multiple missions with different characteristics: arms control verification, humanitarian assistance, and some collective enforcement. Some problems might arise when a peace operation assumes functions that are fundamentally incompatible with one another in terms of the roles, attributes, and behaviors used in the classification. For example, intervention in support of democracy, in which peacekeepers assume primary-party roles in the conflict, may be difficult to achieve simultaneously with another mission that casts peace-keepers as third-party mediators. The local population or the combatants may also have difficulty in deciding whether to cooperate with peace soldiers when they perform divergent and seemingly contradictory missions, such as humanitarian assistance and pacification.

In addition there are important implications for how we understand and account for success in peace operations. Different types of missions might be evaluated with different criteria. For example, monitoring missions might be assessed by their ability to limit armed conflict, whereas emergency missions could be measured by their effect on local populations (see chapter 4 for a full discussion on how to evaluate peace operations). In a related fashion, different factors may account for success or failure across missions, and therefore the "lessons" that one draws from analyzing peace operations may be misguided unless one accounts for these. For example, many analysts have attempted to generalize from US problems in Somalia (UNITAF) or the UN failure in Rwanda (UNAMIR) to future operations, but the implication here is that such attempts may lead to incorrect policies, and ultimately failure, unless the types of missions are the same.

Locating Peace Operations in Different Conflict Phases
Another way to classify and compare peace operations is by the timing of the intervention of troops in the conflict situation. The timing of third-party intervention is thought to be a key component for conflict management success, although exactly when a conflict is "ripe" for settlement is poorly defined or specified. Cold War peacekeeping was generally character-ized by deployment following a ceasefire between disputants but before a final resolution (often indicated by a peace treaty or agreement for elections). More recent operations have

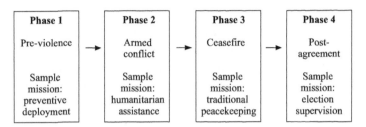

Phase 1		**Phase 2**		**Phase 3**		**Phase 4**
Pre-violence	→	Armed conflict	→	Ceasefire	→	Post-agreement
Sample mission: preventive deployment		Sample mission: humanitarian assistance		Sample mission: traditional peacekeeping		Sample mission: election supervision

Figure 1.1 Phases of conflict

broadened the range of choice for when to intervene. Roughly, there are four different "phases" in which peacekeepers might be initially deployed: pre-violence, during armed conflict, after a ceasefire, and following a peace agreement. Each has different implications for the conduct and success of a peace operation. The timing of deployment is correlated with mission type, as certain operational tasks presume one or more of the four conflict phases being present (see figure 1.1). The timing of intervention is partly within the control of the authorizing agency, but (1) not all conflicts proceed through all phases or do so in a linear fashion, and (2) the timing of deployment may depend on issues of host-state or disputants' consent.

Peace operation deployment in the pre-armed conflict phase, sometimes referred to as "preventive deployment," involves sending troops in anticipation of conflict escalation. The purpose of such forces is to deter violence in the area of deployment and provide a trip-wire that lessens the value to preemptive attacks. Preventive deployments may also implicitly suggest that purpose of such forces is to deter violence in the area of deployment and provide a trip-wire that lessens the value of preemptive attacks. Preventive deployments may also implicitly suggest that, if armed attacks do occur, the organizing agency will respond with greater use of force to stop the conflict or punish the aggressor.

There is strong normative appeal to preventive deployments. If they can deter armed attacks, the local citizenry
clearly benefit the most. Widespread killing, waves of refugees, and dislocations of the economy are avoided. At the
macro-level, preventing violent conflict may make it easier to
promote conflict resolution in the long run, as the increased
hatred and mistrust from war are avoided and the consequences of the armed conflict do not have to be factored into
potential settlements. Thus, from a policymaking perspective,
early intervention is most desirable. Nevertheless, pre-
violence deployment presumes a well-developed and effective
early warning system that permits the accurate prediction of
when and where armed conflict is likely, and therefore when
and where soldiers should be deployed. Unfortunately, such a
system does not yet exist, and there are significant barriers to
its adoption. Furthermore, even given accurate early warning,
there is the presumption that the international political will to
act on such information also exists. Yet states may be offended
by being labeled as sites for potential armed conflict (especially
involving internal conflict), and there are serious sovereignty
issues raised by preventive deployments. In addition, organizations such as the UN or others are notoriously crisis-driven,
and it is difficult to muster political support and resources for
problems that are not yet fully manifest. The United Nations
Preventive Deployment Force (UNPREDEP) is the only true
empirical example of preventive deployment. The purpose of
UNPREDEP, which was essentially an offshoot mission of
UNPROFOR in Bosnia, was to monitor and report any developments in the border areas and deter the spread of conflict
into the former Yugoslav Republic of Macedonia. To its credit,
the expansion of the Bosnian conflict was avoided.

Intervention during the second conflict phase, while
military hostilities are ongoing, is perhaps the most risky.
A traditional peacekeeping force is generally ill-equipped

to be thrust into the middle of active hostilities; it usually does not have the capacity to suppress military conflict and may even be limited in its ability to defend itself. A variety of missions might be performed during this phase, with pacification being the most obvious. Yet, peace operations might also provide humanitarian assistance or protect threatened populations during armed conflict. Deployment in this phase has been very rare in interstate conflicts but represents a significant portion (20 percent) of peace operations in civil wars (Wallensteen and Heldt 2008).

Most prominently, UN peacekeepers attempted to intervene during active fighting in Somalia (UNOSOM II) and Bosnia, and African Union (AMIS) forces have tried to discourage genocide in Sudan. By most standards, these efforts were a failure. The peacekeepers were unable to stop the fighting, were involved in several nasty incidents themselves, and ultimately were withdrawn well short of their goals. Certainly, the operations can be given credit for delivering humanitarian assistance to needy populations in a few cases, although it is unclear whether NGOs might have been equally or more effective in those tasks.

The most familiar timing of deployment is following a ceasefire but before resolution of the underlying disputes between the hostile parties. This is traditional peacekeeping deployment. As noted in the presentation on traditional peacekeeping above, the primary mission in this phase is the maintenance of a ceasefire. Yet, certain other missions, including working with the local population to open transit points and to provide relief services, are possible as well. Many traditional missions fit this profile, including the UNFICYP operation, in place since 1964. This indicates that some conflicts may never, or at least only very slowly, move beyond this third phase.

The world community may no longer wait for conflicts

to reach this third stage before considering peacekeeping deployment. Yet it is clear that ceasefires are a high priority when intervening in the previous conflict phase, and a peace operation may rapidly move from phase 2 (fighting) to phase 3 (ceasefire). Unfortunately, as the Bosnian (UNPROFOR) and Liberian (ECOMOG) experiences demonstrate, it is quite possible to oscillate back and forth between these two phases. It may be more desirable for peace operations to occur after a ceasefire, but clearly the costs of waiting may be high, and there is no guarantee that ceasefires will be negotiated, much less hold once in place.

The final phase of conflict, after a peace settlement is achieved, is in some ways the optimal time for peacekeepers. Yet one must remember that the combatants and the world community may have had to struggle through the other three phases to reach this point. Peace operations may supervise democratic elections and facilitate the implementation of peace agreements. Those in Cambodia (UNTAC) and Namibia (United Nations Transition Assistance Group, UNTAG) are examples of operations that led to free and fair elections, with participation rates well above projections and disruptions below what might have been expected. The Multinational Force and Observers (MFO) in the Sinai have also monitored troop pullbacks and the return of territory stemming from peace agreements between Egypt and Israel.

Peace operations after conflict resolution, however, are by no means foolproof. Some agreements, such as the Dayton Accords for Bosnia, are far from comprehensive agreements. Peace operations in those contexts (e.g., SFOR) may find themselves closer to phase 3 than in an endgame situation. Peace agreements are also not a guarantee of the parties' commitment to the peace process, as evidenced by the Sudanese government's behavior with regard to Darfur. The latest waves of democratization and ethnic conflicts starting in the early 1990s have produced more opportunities for peace operations in this phase; intrastate conflicts and international interventions in said conflicts have constituted the primary threats to international peace and security in the last several decades (Human Security Report Project, 2012). Yet the debacles in Somalia and Bosnia have made states reluctant to assume long-term tasks in nation-building and other post-settlement missions. Finally, initial success may disappear in the long run, after or sometimes even before the peace operations have ended. Democratic elections in Cambodia and Angola have not promoted peace in the long run, no matter how well peacekeepers did their jobs. Indeed, the latter stages of the fourth phase might be conceptualized as the beginning of phase 1, as stability needs to be maintained and is subject to the potential for future conflict (Schnabel 2002).

Peace Operations' Place in Conflict Management and Resolution

Conflict management generally refers to the mitigation of conflict such that its most violent and undesirable consequences are avoided; issue differences and accompanying hostilities between the protagonists may still exist. In contrast, conflict resolution signifies that the disputants have resolved their differences, with little likelihood of future hostilities, violent or otherwise, over stakes that were previously the source of conflict. Peace operations are only one among many strategies designed to promote conflict management and resolution.

In understanding peace operations, it is useful to consider how they relate to other conflict management and resolution strategies. First, peace operations are not necessarily mutually exclusive with respect to those strategies. Indeed, peace operations are sometimes designed to work synergistically with those other approaches. Second, a comparison of strategies is useful for understanding how peace operations might differ in assumptions and execution from other strategies.

Peace operations are predicated on, or at least consistent with, a number of assumptions common to a philosophy of the peaceful settlement of disputes (see Claude 1971). Most notably, the peaceful settlement of disputes presumes that the parties would rather (1) settle a dispute rather than not, and (2) do so without violence. There are circumstances, of course, in which domestic political interests are served by the continuation of conflict, but most disputants do wish to resolve disagreements; the problem is not usually with the willingness to settle but with the conditions of any such settlement. The preference for settlement without violence is based on risk and costs; leaders are thought to be rational, in that they prefer an outcome without the costs of combat over one following a war. Peace operations, especially traditional peace-keeping, typically assume that the parties want peace – many peace missions depend on the cooperation of the parties to maintain ceasefires, to conduct free and fair elections, and to undertake other tasks.

The peaceful settlement of disputes also depends on the presence of viable alternatives to armed conflict. Peace operations are not such alternatives per se and are not designed to be permanent solutions to conflict; rather, they are designed to create space for alternatives. Peace operations are thought to provide the time and a cooling-off period for peaceful alternatives to be devised. As Claude (1971) argues, delay is supposed to be desirable for conflict management and resolution, and peace operations may freeze the status quo or otherwise prevent a march toward the use of armed force. Peace operations might also play the role, especially in the later phases of a conflict, of implementing peaceful alternatives. In this way, they are a facilitating condition for alternatives to military force in solving disputes.

Different conflict management and resolution strategies can broadly be arrayed along a continuum according to the degree of coercion involved (this is also correlated with the degree to which the third party takes an active or a primary role in conflict). At the one extreme are diplomatic alternatives. Chapter VI of the UN Charter provides a useful enumeration of the different alternatives. Among these are negotiation, inquiry, mediation, conciliation, arbitration, and judicial settlement. Each of these strategies has its unique features; yet all parties involved present their competing positions, and a solution is reached either directly by the parties or by an authoritative third party. Peace operations do not necessarily perform any of the same functions as these diplomatic alternatives, or at least to the same end. Peace operation personnel may be involved as mediators or in rendering rulings that resemble arbitration, but these involve micro-issues rather than central issues in the broader dispute. For example, peacekeepers may be called on to negotiate a dispute with a civilian at a roadblock or to render judgment about which side is responsible for a given ceasefire violation. Peace missions are usually separate from broader diplomatic initiatives that seek to manage or resolve the underlying dispute between the hostile parties, even if they share the same organizing agency. Peacebuilding operations often involve greater integration between different actors and tasks, although they too rely on specialization of duties.

Although the activities of peace missions are different from diplomatic strategies, they may be considered consistent with, or even complementary to, those strategies. Peace operations, especially those in the first three phases of conflict, are designed to lessen the chances of violent conflict. In many conceptions, their success may facilitate the proper environment in which diplomatic alternatives can occur and be successful. In the fourth phase, the post-agreement one, peace operations may actually implement settlements precipitated by successful diplomacy. In this way, peace operations follow diplomacy rather than being prerequisites or companions to it.

Chapter VII of the UN Charter outlines strategies toward the more coercive end of the spectrum. Economic sanctions seek to compel one or more disputants to perform or refrain from certain actions. Compellence, rather than persuasion or the provision of positive incentives, is the mechanism for inducing the desired outcome. Peace operations may or may not be compatible with sanctions strategies, depending on the mission. One possible mission is sanctions enforcement, in which peacekeepers might patrol borders or shipping lanes in order to prevent smuggling or actions contrary to sanctions provision.

Peace operations might also be compatible with sanctions to the extent that the two strategies map onto each other with respect to impartiality. If peace operations are not designed to favor any side in a conflict and sanctions are not targeted toward one protagonist over another (for example, a blanket arms embargo that on the surface applies to all parties), then the two approaches are compatible, even complementary, if the goal is to limit the scope of violence. Yet, if the sponsoring organization has imposed sanctions against one party (for example, a government in a civil conflict) while simultaneously launching a peace operation that is designed to be impartial, problems may arise. Protagonists may not distinguish between the unbiased actions of the organizing agency and its broader political positions in enacting sanctions, and therefore an attack on peacekeepers, as occurred in Bosnia, may be the result.

At the far end of the spectrum are highly coercive mechanisms that are often grouped under the rubric of "collective security." Collective security actions are military operations that seek to impose a solution, temporary or more long term, to a threat to international peace and security. Collective security operations are fundamentally different from traditional peacekeeping operations, but some newer peace operations have begun to assume some of the characteristics of more coercive operations.

The differences between military forces and traditional peacekeeping are highlighted above. Beyond those distinctions, collective security has a fundamentally different orientation from traditional peacekeeping. Collective security operations presume that a given side in a conflict can be labeled as the aggressor and therefore the target of military action.[6] Traditional peacekeeping does not assign blame to any one party. Collective security involves large-scale military action to repel or defeat the aggressor. Peacekeeping offers limited military action, with only defensive use of force permitted. Collective security is designed to take place during the second phase of conflict, when active fighting occurs; indeed, a collective of states participates in the ongoing war. Traditional peacekeeping has historically been located in the third phase, after active hostilities have been terminated. Although neither approach is designed to promote political change itself, collective security is also designed to restore the status quo ante – that is, the situation before the outbreak of hostilities. In contrast, traditional peacekeeping freezes the status quo at the time of the deployment; this may or may not be the same as the status quo ante in terms of territorial acquisition or other issues of contention. Both strategies give preference to peaceful methods as the mechanisms for permanent changes in territory or resolution of disputes. Unlike other conflict management and resolution alternatives, it is contradictory to deploy a traditional peacekeeping force and a collective security operation simultaneously, although the former could follow the latter; for example, NATO troops performed peace operation functions following the successful repulsion of Yugoslav military forces from Kosovo.

Over time, as noted more fully in the next chapter, some peace operations have evolved to take on more coercive missions, which some commentators have labeled "Chapter VI1/2" operations, signifying their place on the continuum between the diplomatic approaches outlined in Chapter VI of the UN Charter and the highly coercive actions envisioned in Chapter VII. Those peace operations are not the same as collective security, but force size is increased, offensive military actions are included, and military action may be directed primarily against one or more of the combatants.

Peace operations are part of the set of conflict management and resolution strategies open to the international community. They may occupy various positions on the coercive continuum between purely diplomatic actions and collective security operations. In most cases, they are best seen as supplements or complements to other approaches rather than as substitutable options. The reasons for this come out of the unique historical development of peace operations, which is detailed in the next chapter.

CHAPTER TWO

The Historical Evolution and Record of Peace Operations

The origin and development of peace operations largely parallel those of international organizations in general. Yet, the traditional peacekeeping strategy evolved specifically out of experience with peace observation missions and the failure of collective security under the League of Nations and the United Nations. This chapter traces the historical development of peace operations from their earliest manifestations to the emergence of post-Cold War peacebuilding.[1] The chapter concludes with an overview of peace operations since 1945.

Early International Efforts

Whereas war and other organized violence have a long history, actions by the international community to promote peace are far more recent. The earliest incidence of collective military action at the international level might be the Crusades. In that instance, several states banded together, with the encouragement of the Vatican, to save the Holy Land from the scourges of those who were regarded as pagans. Yet, unlike their modern-day successors, these actions were hardly designed to restore peace and security, and one also could argue that they were not coordinated under provisions set up by a global or regional intergovernmental organization.

The Crusades proved not to set a precedent. In the fourteenth century came a proposal, never actualized, for a world government that included arrangements for an international army. After the Napoleonic Wars in the nineteenth century, the major powers acted together (the Concert of Europe) to preserve the status quo, and this embraced collective (broadly construed) military action that, again, only faintly resembled the organized and internationally sanctioned operations that would occur in the next century. The closest analogue to peace operations before the establishment of the League of Nations occurred in 1849–50, when a Norwegian–Swedish force of 3,800 troops was deployed in Schleswig as part of an armistice that was agreed upon in July 1849 between Denmark and Prussia during the First Schleswig War. "The task was to maintain law, order, and justice in northern Schleswig under observance of the strictest neutrality between Danes and Germans" (Gäfvert, 1995: 31). This international force, which "might not take part in the hostilities" (ibid.) if the armistice were to be cancelled, remained deployed until peace was agreed in July 1850.

Early international efforts at collective military action shared a number of characteristics. First, they operated on an ad hoc basis, organizing and disbanding as the need arose and according to the crisis at hand. This attribute persists in international peace operations to this day. Second, beyond the ad hoc arrangements, these early actions had little precedent to follow. Thus, they operated without specific guidelines, often with little coordination between national units. This circumstance would change in the twentieth century, when peace operations relied heavily on guidelines established by previous operations in terms of personnel, deployment, and conduct. Finally, early efforts went forward in most cases largely without the approval or the direction of an international body, because international organizations as we know them today did not exist. The protection of international peace and security was largely indistinguishable from the interests of the major powers in the world – a condition that would change, at least organizationally, with the creation of an appropriate international mechanism for authorizing and coordinating global security actions.[2]

The League of Nations Experience: Collective Security
The end of World War I and the desire by the global community to make that truly "the war to end all wars" led to the formation of the first general-purpose, universal membership organization – the League of Nations. Although that organization had economic and social functions as well, its primary purpose was to ensure international peace and security through collective consultation and action. In the course of drafting the League of Nations Covenant, France proposed that military sanctions be executed by an international force. The British and US delegations objected to this provision, and accordingly it is absent from Articles 10 and 16 of that document. Nevertheless, those articles do outline, in broad form, collective security procedures. Article 10 states: "The Members of the League undertake to respect and preserve as against external aggression the territorial integrity and existing political independence of all Members of the League. In case of any such aggression ... the Council shall advise upon the means by which this obligation shall be fulfilled."

The provisions of that article are a far cry from installing discretionary power in an international police force to meet threats to international security. Yet Article 16 is less equivocal in outlining the possible international military response to aggression:

> Should any Member resort to war ... it shall ipso facto be deemed to have committed an act of war against all other Members. ... It shall be the duty of the Council in such case to recommend to the several Governments concerned what effective military, naval, or air force the Members of the

> League shall severally contribute to the armed forces to be
> used to protect the covenants of the League.

These provisions supplied the legal authority for the League to take collective military action, only one option at the disposal of the Council. Furthermore, the operations were to be organized on an ad hoc basis, much as were their historical predecessors. Finally, military operations would probably be neither under the control of the League nor involve truly international forces. There is enough ambiguity in the language of the articles and sufficient political reasons to believe that the military actions would be loosely coordinated national efforts undertaken by the major powers with the approval of the League.

The collective security procedures of the League of Nations were not tested until more than a decade after the inception of the organization. In 1931, Japan attacked Manchuria and occupied the capital city; China appealed to the Council of the League for assistance. Over the objections of Japan, the Council recommended withdrawal of the Japanese troops; yet stronger actions under Article 11 of the League Covenant would necessitate a unanimous vote, a result unlikely because of the potential Japanese veto. This state of affairs all but precluded forceful action against any of the members, a problem that foreshadowed similar difficulties with the superpowers in the United Nations.

Rather than stiff economic sanctions or an international military action against Japan, the League was able to authorize only a fact-finding mission to the area. During the long process of inquiry, Japan set up the puppet state of Manchukuo and directed its aggressive eye toward the rest of China. By the time the fact-finding report was presented to the League, Japanese aggression had borne its full fruits, and it was impossible to undo the harvest. Japan added insult to this ineffectiveness by withdrawing from the organization.

The next major test of the League's collective action mechanisms would yield only slightly better results. Italy attacked Ethiopia in 1935 and ultimately conquered that country, for which the League instituted economic sanctions against Italy. Yet, many of the League members, as well as the United States, either failed to institute those sanctions fully or blatantly ignored them. The major downfall of the League's actions against Italy was the British and French willingness to recognize Italian domination over parts of North Africa. Britain and France mistakenly thought that appeasing Italy would lead that country to recognize British and French interests on the African continent and perhaps secure them an ally against rising Nazi power in Germany. The willingness of major powers to place their own interests ahead of those of the international community again foreshadowed Cold War tensions and the paralysis of the United Nations in coming decades.

The League of Nations Experience: Peace Observation and Inquiry

Despite the failure of its collective security arrangements, the League of Nations was active in several disputes and crises. During these disputes, it began to perform some peace observation functions that were to evolve into the traditional peacekeeping strategy in later years. The League Covenant makes no mention of peace observation, yet Article 11, authorizing the League to "take any action that may be deemed wise and effectual to safeguard the peace of nations," opened the door to actions not specifically mentioned in the Covenant or envisioned by its authors. Furthermore, Article 15 provided for the Council to report on the facts of disputes and make recommendations on how those disputes might be settled peacefully. These two articles would form the basis for League actions that combined the missions of fact finding and observation.

The first League action came very early in the life of the organization. A dispute between Sweden and Finland over the Aaland Islands led the League to create a commission of inquiry to investigate the situation and recommend solutions. At first glance, a fact-finding mission would seem to offer few precedents for future peace observation. Indeed, this dispute was not so severe as to suggest that military conflict was imminent or even likely. Yet this simple case established a precedent that the League could successfully intervene in a dispute and act in a neutral fashion in pursuit of a peaceful solution. The acceptance, albeit without enthusiasm, of the fact-finding report by the protagonists also helped establish the League's reputation as a fair arbiter.

Throughout the 1920s, the League involved itself in a number of disputes. The usual method was to create fact-finding commissions that would report back to the Council, following the strategy outlined in the Covenant and the precedent established in the Aaland Islands case. In the dispute between Poland and Germany over Upper Silesia, troops were sent to supervise the plebiscite in the area. Yet these were hardly international troops, as France, Italy, and later Britain sent and retained control over their own forces. Furthermore, these could not be considered neutral forces, in that the sponsoring countries each had interests and supported a particular outcome of the dispute. Although such action did not resemble later peace observation missions, it did represent a key instance of the use of internationally sanctioned forces in a supervisory role.

The Greek–Bulgarian crisis of 1925 provided a further opportunity for League involvement and the establishment of another precedent that would later form the basis of peace observation and peacekeeping missions. Before the Council authorized a fact-finding mission, it insisted that there be a ceasefire, which was subsequently achieved. This became a virtual requirement for authorizing a traditional peacekeeping operation. Among the recommendations of the commission of inquiry was the pullback of forces and their separation at a safe distance, supervised by neutral observers. A committee composed of representatives from both disputants and some neutral parties, including a League chair, was to discuss problems with the ceasefire and limit the escalation potential of hostile incidents. The construction of a buffer zone and the establishment of such a committee became standard operating procedures for traditional peacekeeping operations.

Shortly after the Aaland Islands dispute, a more serious conflict arose between Poland and Lithuania over the province of Vilna. More than just deploying a fact-finding mission this time, the League was successful in negotiating a provisional line of demarcation and a neutral, demilitarized zone between the disputants, thus setting the physical and political conditions for the introduction of an international force.

An international force of 1,500 from states that had no seat on the Council (in marked contrast to that in Upper Silesia) was designed to replace irregular Polish troops that occupied the disputed territory and to supervise a plebiscite in the area. Unfortunately, such a force never assumed those roles. First, both disputants, and Lithuania in particular, placed roadblocks in the way of League efforts, illustrating the difficulty (or perhaps impossibility) of neutral international intervention without the cooperation of the disputants. Furthermore, major power interests made Council action both within and outside the League rather difficult. Although this case was successful in that war was ultimately avoided, peace observation was thwarted by the non-cooperation of the parties involved and major power disagreements. Nevertheless, this failure would prove to be a stepping stone in the successful deployment of an international force in the Saar, which may be the League model closest to present-day observation or peace forces.

The League of Nations action in the Saar may be the first true example of an international peace observation force. Yet, the conditions under which the operation functioned were extraordinary and, indeed, helped contribute to the success of the mission. The Saar, lying between France and Germany, was to be an internationally administered territory for a period of years following World War I, at which time a plebiscite would decide the final disposition of the area, with options including unification with France or Germany. Thus, the usual problem of obtaining permission of the host country for the stationing of an international force was not an issue in this case: the League was the equivalent of the host state. This became particularly important when Germany made several hostile gestures toward the establishment of the force. The French were also less than fully cooperative, perhaps believing (correctly) that the territory would ultimately be returned to Germany. The international administration of territories would be repeated decades later by the UN in East Timor and NATO in Kosovo.

The Saar force was made up of troops from Britain, Italy, and other European countries – not exactly a neutral force in its composition, but the way it was commanded represented a significant advance. Unlike previous missions, in which nations maintained control of units, this force was under the direction of the League through an appointed commander. Although the troops were to maintain order before and during the plebiscite, they did not function as an international police force. They patrolled the territory, but would take action only in emergency situations, and then only in response to a request by the local authorities. The level of military force was to be kept at a minimum, reflecting what would become the standard for limitations on the use of military force in peace missions. Despite some threats from local officials and the massing of German troops near the border of the disputed territory, the operation was a success, with little or no violence.

The Saar expedition is important not only because it represented the first truly international force, but also because the report of its commander, General Brind, contained several recommendations that would become centerpieces of observation and traditional peacekeeping strategy in the future. Among his recommendations was that troops in future operations be drawn from countries that had no direct interest in the dispute, all but guaranteeing that major power forces would not be involved. Brind also noted that only a small number of troops were necessary to complete the mission, and that it was the moral influence of the Saar force rather than any direct action that was responsible for successfully deterring trouble in the disputed area. These two elements underline the absence of an enforcement capability and identify the prevailing strategy in preserving peace, in contrast to collective security actions. This legacy would be manifest in peacekeeping operations two decades later.[3]

Early United Nations Experience

The UN provisions for conflict intervention resemble those of the League but are laid out more explicitly and rely on an increasingly coercive sequence of actions. As noted in chapter 1, the UN Charter provides a number of dispute resolution alternatives to the use of military force. Beyond such options as mediation and judicial settlement, the United Nations, through the Security Council, is empowered to investigate the dispute (Article 34) and recommend means (Article 36) or terms (Articles 37 and 38) of settlement. This was largely the mode of operation for the League of Nations – inquiry and conciliation. Yet, when it came to the use of force, the United Nations had both the rationale and the mechanisms to take collective action.

Chapter VII of the UN Charter lists some courses of action for UN members to take should peaceful methods of settlement outlined in Chapter VI fail. Reliance on sanctions, the tack taken against Iraq following its invasion of Kuwait, might fail, and the Security Council might need to authorize the use of military force. Article 42 directly identifies the collective security option: "[the Security Council] may take such action by air, sea, or land forces as may be necessary to maintain or restore international peace and security."

In one sense, the UN strategy and mechanisms for dealing with threats to international peace and security were similar to those that had achieved little success under the League. Many of the initial options centered on the Security Council making suggestions for resolution of the dispute after some deliberation and inquiry. The collective security option was also a last resort, although again the autonomy of the organization was limited to specific authorizations by its members. Surprisingly, the Charter did not mention the notion of peace observation, and peacekeeping operations were yet to be created. International organizations still lacked formal options between enforcement measures and diplomacy.

Under the League, the Council required unanimity before authorizing certain actions under Article 11, which effectively limited the range of actions directed against one of the Council members. The UN Security Council voting system requires only nine of fifteen votes to take action, provided none of the five permanent members of the Council (the United States, the Soviet Union – now Russia, China, the United Kingdom, and France) opposes the resolution. Thus the United Nations replaced unanimity among all members under the League with the requirement for acquiescence among the most important subset of its members – the major powers. This was designed to ensure that the latter would be united (thought to be a necessity for concerted global action) and to make decisions for action somewhat easier than in the League.

Beyond a change in the voting system to authorize peace and security action, the UN Charter included the infrastructure to carry out that action. First, it provided for a Military Staff Committee (Article 47) that was "responsible . . . for the strategic direction of any armed forces placed at the disposal of the Security Council." Although actual command of such forces was deferred until a later time, establishing the Military Staff Committee was the United Nations' effort to have a direct say in the conduct of forces on an international mission. It also assumed continuity of action and the establishment of procedures for the use and conduct of those forces. The committee was designed to be a significant step forward from the purely ad hoc national efforts thought to characterize League of Nations actions.

Yet the provisions for supply of troops remained distinctly ad hoc. Article 43 provides: "All Members of the United Nations . . . undertake to make available to the Security Council, on its call and in accordance with a special agreement or agreements, armed forces, assistance, and facilities, including rights of passage, necessary for the purpose of maintaining international peace and security." Similar to the League, the United Nations would not have its own military forces but would have to rely on the contributions of its members, although the command of those forces would now be under the control of the international organization. Nevertheless, that some national troops were at least earmarked for duty in the UN was an advancement over League practice.

Even though the United Nations made adjustments based on the League of Nations experience, the net results did not differ dramatically with respect to collective security. Changing the voting system from one of unanimity to one based on a major power veto only perpetuated the stalemate of the League's Council; the veto provision prevented the Security Council from taking meaningful action against any of the major powers. By confining the Security Council to operations against or involving states other than the major powers, and given that major powers have global interests and that their disputes provide the greatest threat to international security, this limitation is substantial.

Yet, even in the case of minor power disputes, the veto proved a strong impediment to action. The rapid escalation of the Cold War after World War II increasingly polarized the international system. Few states could be said not to belong to the camp of one superpower or the other. Thus, when faced with a crisis in Iran or Turkey, for example, the Security Council was stifled by the veto of one of the superpowers. The development of proxy wars in the Middle East and elsewhere made it virtually impossible for the United Nations to take any strong action. Even though unanimity was not required, the presence of the veto had the same effect, and the United Nations took little strong action in the area of peace and security.

For many of the same reasons as in the League of Nations, the UN attempt to develop a better mechanism for carrying out collective security operations was also a failure. Earmarking troops for UN service may have been a good idea, but it depended on successfully negotiating the initial agreements to provide those forces. Unfortunately, Cold War disagreements prevented states from ever coming to resolution on that matter, destroying what little advantage might have been achieved. Furthermore, the Military Staff Committee never lived up to expectations. With no operations to supervise, and no troops readily available in any case, it quickly became moribund, and the United Nations found itself squarely back where the League of Nations had ended, with neither the will nor the mechanisms to launch enforcement actions. Before the United Nations turned to peacekeeping, however, it performed its first collective security operation, in Korea.

During the early 1950s it might seem at first glance that the Korean situation would establish an important precedent for collective security actions. Were this the case, the strategy of peacekeeping might never have emerged. Instead, the Korean intervention was almost a one-shot wonder. In subsequent conflicts, the aggressor was not so clearly evident. The problem becomes even more complex when dealing with internal conflicts in which the United Nations might be forced to defend a rather offensive status quo, such as apartheid South Africa. In addition, the Soviet absence from the Council during deliberations over the Korean War, which facilitated the passage of the initial resolutions, has not been repeated; all the major powers have been careful to leave at least one representative even during a symbolic walkout.

After little more than a decade of existence, the United Nations found itself stalled by many of the same forces that had crippled the League of Nations. Disagreements among the major powers and the lack of appropriate mechanisms once again made collective security an unrealized dream. Nevertheless, peace operations developed quickly out of the precedents set by the failure of collective security and the success of early UN peace observation missions.

UN Peace Observation
The United Nations continued the tradition of peace observation that had begun under the League of Nations. As collective security proved unworkable, these missions provided the new organization with experience in conflict intervention and, in a few instances, offered guidelines that would be adopted under

peacekeeping.

Civil instability in Greece after World War II provided the first opportunity for peace observation. In line with League experience, a UN fact-finding mission was dispatched. Yet, because Greek communists were involved in the civil unrest, the conflict became part of the emerging Cold War at the international level. As a result of the Soviet veto in the Security Council, the General Assembly had to take the lead and set up an observation force, with posts at the Greek borders with Albania, Yugoslavia, and Bulgaria. The force did not maintain continuous supervision of the border areas, as would a traditional peacekeeping force, but did make frequent inspections to discourage the supply of rebel troops from abroad. The mission was largely a success, in that Greece was stabilized, but there were various complaints, especially concerning the Albanian border and the covert supply of guerrilla forces. Nevertheless, this mission demonstrated that peace observation could function (1) in a Cold War dispute and (2) when stationed on only one side of a border.

The first UN attempt at truce supervision was in assisting Indonesian independence from the Netherlands. Observers were placed at the disposal of the "good offices" commission that was trying to negotiate a peaceful withdrawal of Dutch forces from Indonesia. The main purpose of that peace observation was to provide a calm atmosphere under which mediation efforts might succeed. Having secured an agreement for the independence of Indonesia, the observers later monitored the demobilization and withdrawal of Dutch forces, another function that peace operations would later acquire.

Following the 1948 war in the Middle East, the UN Truce Supervision Organization (UNTSO) was charged with observing the truce and agreed-upon limitations on the movement of troops and materiel. Although this type of activity seems to resemble later peacekeeping operations in the region, the initial impression is misleading. The observation mission had only a small number of personnel (fewer than 600) and dealt mostly with responding to complaints from the parties. Various hostile incidents followed its initial deployment in 1948 and, later, the breakdown of order in the region during the Suez Crisis. UNTSO also had difficulties because of its vague mandate, the ill-defined boundaries between Jordan and Israel, and the large number of refugees moving through the region.

The United Nations also sent an observer mission a few years after World War II to another trouble spot. In conjunction with a fact-finding and mediation mission that achieved a ceasefire in 1949, a UN team (UNMOGIP) was dispatched to Kashmir, in the center of the Indo-Pakistani conflict, and was stationed with regular Indian and Pakistani troops. The observer force, which remains in place today, has investigated complaints, provided information on troop movements and actions, and helped local authorities to maintain order. India has scaled back its cooperation with the force and has tried to ignore its presence, and UNMOGIP no longer serves as an important conduit for resolving differences over Kashmir.

The failure of collective security demonstrated the limitations of the United Nations in dealing with threats to international peace and security. The early UN peace observation missions were an attempt to fill the void left by collective security. The mixed record of peace observation and the new challenge of the Suez Crisis led the organization to seek a new strategy. It was in that 1956 crisis that traditional peacekeeping as we know it was born.

UNEF I and the First "Golden Age" of UN Peacekeeping

The Suez Crisis prompted a fundamental change in thinking about the UN role in and mechanisms for dealing with active threats to international peace and security. This change of thinking was necessary before the international community could even contemplate peacebuilding roles years later. In June 1956, the British handed over control of the Suez Canal to Egypt. A little more than a month later, President Nasser nationalized the canal, setting off the Suez Crisis. UN and other diplomatic efforts failed to resolve differences between Israel, Egypt, Britain, and France. The Security Council was paralyzed as the Soviet Union vetoed what some might regard as a compromise resolution and others as pro-Western. Israel invaded Egypt on October 29, setting off the second Arab–Israeli war in a decade. One day later, Britain and France issued an ultimatum to Egypt and Israel demanding that forces be moved away from the canal and that British and French troops fill the void to ensure free passage. Egypt rejected this ultimatum.

Because of the stalemate in the Security Council, the General Assembly faced a situation in which peace observation was inadequate to the task but collective enforcement was politically impossible. Furthermore, Britain and France

---

Box 2.1 UNEF I

UNEF I was charged with monitoring the ceasefire between forces and supervising the withdrawal of the forces of France, United Kingdom, and Israel from the area. After this withdrawal, UNEF was tasked to serve as a buffer between the Egyptian and Israeli forces.

Headquarters: Gaza

Duration: November 1956 – June 1967

Maximum strength: 6,037

Cost: US$214.2 million

insisted on some sort of international police force before they withdrew their troops. On November 4, 1956, the General Assembly passed the seminal Resolution 998, which authorized the Secretary-General to set up a UN force to be dispatched to the region.

Specifically, the United Nations Emergency Force (UNEF I) was charged with monitoring the ceasefire between forces and supervising the withdrawal of these forces from the area. It later acted as a buffer against the future engagement of Arab and Israeli forces. Importantly, its mission was limited to these functions. It played no role in reopening or in the delicate negotiations that followed concerning the management of the canal, in contrast to the fact-finding and conciliation functions often tied to peace observation. Although limited in mandate, UNEF I was a dramatic innovation: armed international soldiers were now charged with specific functions in an interstate conflict, including monitoring troop withdrawal.

The period from 1956 (the advent of the UNEF I operation) until 1978 is popularly known as the first "golden age" of peacekeeping. This is because it was the period during the Cold War in which the greatest number of peacekeeping operations were authorized. In these two decades, the UN deployed ten new peacekeeping or observation missions to different areas of the world. Although some areas were excluded (the superpower spheres of influence), traditional peacekeeping and observation was the predominant operational method by which the international community responded to threats to international peace and security.

With the notable exception of the Congo operation (see below), most peacekeeping operations in this period shared a number of characteristics, in contrast to contemporary peacebuilding operations. These operations were put in place before any peace settlement but following a ceasefire; this is consistent with earlier peace observation missions. The UN was still not focused on preventive mechanisms. The duties of the peacekeeping forces were very limited. Traditional peace-keepers acted as interposition forces, separating combatants in order to deter military engagements. They also monitored ceasefires and helped resolve any disputes that arose over the terms of the halt in fighting. Additional activities, such as clearing transportation routes and providing medical assistance to local populations, occurred, but they tended to be incidental, certainly not part of the mandate granted to them by the UN Security Council. Traditional peacekeeping operations were also deployed almost exclusively in inter-state conflicts, quite unlike the peacebuilding operations that would occur decades later.

If traditional peacekeeping operations in the first golden age were so different from peacebuilding missions, what role did the former play in stimulating the latter? It was certainly not the tasks that the peacekeepers performed. Rather, these series of operations routinized and legitimized the norm of the international community intervening in international conflicts. Collective security actions were moribund, and peace observation missions were still infrequent. Traditional peacekeeping became the baseline response to threats to inter-national peace, albeit only ones that did not directly involve either of the superpowers. The fundamental characteristics of traditional operations (lightly armed and impartial forces) would later be modified according to new threats to peace. The important point is that peacebuilding operations were not created *de novo*, but rather as deviations from the traditional peacekeeping profile.

Perhaps the most significant exception to the norm of tra-ditional peacekeeping operations was the United Nations Operation in the Congo (ONUC), from 1960 to 1964. It was quite different from other operations in this era and may have foreshadowed later peacebuilding operations. Yet it may have had the paradoxical effects of setting some precedents, as well as forestalling an earlier move to peacebuilding missions.

The Congo Operation: A Proto-Peacebuilding Operation?

The UN operation in the Congo (ONUC) was, in several ways, a very different operation from all other peacekeeping missions in this era.[4] The collapse of law and order following Congolese independence led the Belgian government to deploy troops in order to protect Belgian nationals. At the same time, the province of Katanga declared itself independent from the Congo, apparently with some support from Belgium. The United Nations organized ONUC and dispatched it to the capital city to help ensure the territorial integrity of the Congo, assist in restoring law and order, and supervise the withdrawal of Belgian forces. ONUC was not deployed following a peace settlement but in the middle of active combat. Nevertheless, this operation is perhaps the first instance in which UN peace-keeping troops (as opposed to observers) were sent to a civil war. Previously, peace operations were confined largely to interstate conflicts. The exceptions were mixed cases involving decolonization, but these still affected extant states. The Congo operation also involved decolonization, and the presence of Belgian troops was a motivating factor for UN intervention; yet UN troops stayed after the Belgian withdrawal and were intimately embroiled in what was a struggle between different factions for control of Katanga and indeed the country as a whole. Involvement in civil conflicts is now the most common context for peacebuilding, but the Congo operation was really a convention-breaking operation and opened the door for international actions that seemed to violate the principle of exclusive state sovereignty.

Several of the initial and subsequent actions by ONUC

Box 2.2 ONUC

ONUC was initially tasked to help ensure the territorial integrity of the Congo, assist in restoring law and order, and supervise the withdrawal of Belgian forces. In 1961, several new tasks were added to its mandate: the use of force, if necessary, to prevent the occurrence of civil war, to halt all military operations conducted by Congolese or foreign troops, to arrange for a ceasefire, and to detain and deport all foreign military personnel not affiliated with the United Nations and all mercenaries.

Headquarters: Kinshasa

Duration: July 1960 – June 1964

Maximum strength: 19,828

Cost: US$400.1 million

were similar to later peacebuilding activities and far from the narrow mandate of ceasefire monitoring granted to traditional operations. First, ONUC troops were sent to Katanga with the job of restoring order and facilitating the withdrawal of Belgian troops. This was similar to some peacebuilding actions in which troops perform some civilian police functions and monitor the disarmament of local forces.

When the civil war spread beyond Katanga, ONUC's mandate was expanded to include reconvening the Congolese parliament. The revised mandate also allowed the United Nations to use offensive military force as a last resort in order to prevent an all-out civil war. The United Nations established a conciliation commission to find a way to make peace between the warring factions. ONUC succeeded in obtaining a ceasefire between the parties, as well as an agreement on a new unified government for the country. In a limited way, ONUC was assisting in creating government machinery to run the country after its withdrawal, something later peacebuilding operations would attempt as well. Katanga remained in rebellion, and the United Nations expanded the mandate of ONUC even further, authorizing it to use all means necessary, including military force, to control Katanga. ONUC launched offensive military actions in Katanga and seized most of the province. The UN never operated government machinery or provided the services, as it would in later peacebuilding operations; but nevertheless ONUC was the principal mechanism for establishing local order until a peace agreement finally held and the central government was strong enough to take over in 1964.

In some ways, ONUC was a precedent-setting operation. It established that the United Nations could intervene in civil conflicts and that UN peacekeepers could perform functions far beyond those connected with ceasefire monitoring. Many of the activities represent limited versions of what we associate now with peacebuilding. Nevertheless, disagreements between the major powers (primarily the United States, the Soviet Union, and France) over the Congo operation and the backlash from newly independent African states led the United Nations and the nascent Organization of African Unity away from trying to duplicate the Congo operation in other civil conflicts. Indeed, it would be almost twenty-five years before the UN would again venture into peacekeeping that involved civil conflicts and quasi-peacebuilding actions.

The "Lost Decade" and the Thawing of the Cold War

If the period from the onset of UNEF I until the deployment of UNIFIL (United Nations Interim Force in Lebanon, first authorized in 1978) in southern Lebanon could be called the first golden age of peacekeeping, the ten years that followed (1979–88) might easily be referred to as the "lost decade." No new UN peace operations were deployed during this time, and many observers regarded peacekeeping in general as moribund – the latter is probably incorrect because previously authorized operations in Cyprus and the Middle East continued to operate and were generally successful at conflict abatement. Nevertheless, few would have predicted the development of expansive peacebuilding operations on the horizon.

The lost decade might be attributable to a number of different factors. First, much of the so-called demand for peace operations came from conflicts in which it was least likely to be authorized. Conflicts in Afghanistan, Panama, Grenada, and the like directly involved the superpowers, and traditional peacekeeping was generally excluded from conflicts within the superpowers' spheres of influence. Second, ongoing hotspots (e.g., India–Pakistan, Arab–Israeli) were already covered by one or more UN peacekeeping and observation missions. Third, renewed Cold War tensions in the early 1980s and dissatisfaction with extant operations made peacekeeping a less attractive option during this period.

Toward the end of the 1980s, the logjam would be broken, and a flood of UN and other peace operations would emerge in the next two decades. Auguring the development of peace operations were several new ventures, most notably in Namibia but also elsewhere, that involved election supervision. This was not necessarily a completely new idea, as League of Nations observers previously monitored plebiscites. Still, these operations were a gateway to the establishment of peacebuilding operations.

The United Nations operation in Namibia (United Nations Transition Assistance Group, or UNTAG) exhibited in a limited fashion many of the peacebuilding characteristics noted above. First, it was deployed following a peace agreement between different groups (both local actors and the South African government) in the fourth phase of conflict. Heretofore, peace operations occurred prior to peacemaking. Forces would now be charged with the implementation of an agreement, usually a first step or prerequisite for more expansive peacebuilding activities. Second, UNTAG carried out

several activities associated with peacebuilding – most notably, monitoring disarmament and supervising the electoral
process. Unlike later peacebuilding efforts, however, UNTAG
did not have full control over these functions. The small
number of troops (approximately 4,000) was inadequate to
monitor troop movements and repatriation efforts, especially
early in the process. Furthermore, South African forces maintained some control over the country until election day as
well as during portions of the election process. In addition,
Namibia was not really a purely intrastate conflict but merged
together concerns with decolonization and foreign intervention, as well as internal conflict. All parties consented to the
operation, something more akin to traditional peacekeeping
than some peacebuilding missions. Nevertheless, despite
such problems, most regard the outcome of the Namibian
election as free and fair, and perhaps this is why international
decision-makers sought to repeat and expand this role in
future operations.

The Namibian success would spawn similar operations,
sometimes with more expansive activities. In 1989 and 1990,
the UN Observer Group in Central America (ONUCA) monitored the military disengagement of opposing forces before
and following elections in Nicaragua. More significant was
the United Nations Transitional Authority in Cambodia
(UNTAC). Its name was indicative of the broader powers
and functions assigned to the operation. Much like the
Namibian operation, it was a post-settlement mission in an
internationalized civil conflict, and its centerpiece was to be
supervising elections, which would follow supervised disarmament of various protagonists. Nevertheless, UNTAC was
another incremental step toward contemporary peacebuilding
because of its other characteristics.

UNTAC did not merely monitor elections in a passive fashion. It had the mandate of repatriating refugees, maintaining

law and order, and conducting some governmental functions. Furthermore, it was charged with authority to construct the election system, register voters, and conduct the election, not merely to deter or report on election-day irregularities. Mirroring later peacebuilding operations, UNTAC was supplemented by 7,000 additional UN personnel, most notably civilian police who supervised local police and investigated human rights abuses.

What began in 1978 as the seeming death of peacekeeping was transformed into what is now referred to as its second golden age ten to fifteen years later. "Peacebuilding" was not yet the term used to describe these new forms of peacekeeping, but many of the aspects of peacebuilding were nevertheless already in place by the time of the Cambodia operation. Peacebuilding, however, would reach fruition with the Somalia mission and several other post-Cold War operations.

Somalia and the Birth of Peacebuilding

Many trace the first use of the term "peacebuilding" to the first edition of Boutros-Ghali's *An agenda for peace*, released in 1992. In that book, he may have coined the phrase, but he also described some peacebuilding activities as well as distinguished peacebuilding from other kinds of peace operations, such as traditional peacekeeping and peacemaking (see chapter 1). Although some peacebuilding elements really precede this date, many regard US and UN actions in Somalia as the first, true peacebuilding operations. Other such operations, often with expanded duties, would follow in Bosnia, Haiti, and elsewhere; but Somalia was a watershed moment for peacebuilding.

The UN Operation in Somalia (UNOSOM) was first deployed in 1992 in response to the breakdown of order in

Box 2.3 UNOSOM I

UNOSOM I was established to monitor the ceasefire in Mogadishu and to protect and provide security to both the UN personnel and humanitarian aid convoys.

Headquarters: Mogadishu

Duration: April 1992 – March 1993

Maximum strength: 947 (893 soldiers and 54 military observers)

Cost: US$42.9 million

that country and a humanitarian crisis of colossal proportions. Phase I of the operation was superseded later that year by Operation Restore Hope, an American-led military operation designed to guarantee the distribution of food and medical supplies. UNOSOM II, deployed in 1993, facilitated the transition of peacekeeping and relief duties from a US-centered operation to a UN-directed one; this lasted until early 1995, when the last UN peacekeeping personnel were withdrawn.

United States and United Nations efforts in Somalia went beyond election supervision missions in Namibia and Cambodia, even as Somalia involved no electoral process. First, the Somali crisis was purely internal – at least to the extent that no other state was militarily involved in the country or responsible for a broader threat to international peace and security. Earlier operations in Cambodia and Namibia also included the involvement of powerful neighbors (an interstate component), and international responses to those conflicts therefore had regional security as part of their impetus. Except for some concern about refugees, there were few "negative externalities" associated with the Somali conflict. Indeed, the collapse of the Somali state had the desirable effect of suspending its militarized rivalry with Ethiopia. Second, on a related point, the Somali crisis was primarily a humanitarian one. That is, the international community was motivated more by concerns for "human security" than it was by traditional security matters. Appropriately, peacebuilding strategies were consistent with this motivation, whereas missions involving interposition forces or even election supervision, heretofore the staple of peace operations, would do little to address the suffering taking place in Somalia.

Third, the operations lacked host-state consent, largely because in the face of state collapse there was no national government to give its approval. Fourth, the Somali operation provided for more intrusive peacebuilding activities, perhaps because of the absence of a central government authority. These activities involved emergency relief (in terms of distribution of food and medical supplies) as well as trying to establish law and order in the country. Local reconciliation efforts between different factions were part of this larger task. UN operations also involved greater coordination with NGOs, heretofore less common in peace operations and more typical of pure humanitarian assistance activities.

The evolution of peace operations continued after Somalia. The second golden age of peacekeeping may have ended shortly after the genocide in Rwanda and the failure of the UN and its members to prevent it. Still, Rwanda had more the effect of causing UN members to be reluctant to enter conflicts at all, or to do so only after certain conditions were present – note the unwillingness of the Security Council to authorize troops for the Congo in the 1990s or the Darfur region of Sudan until those areas were stabilized. The retrenchment, however, does not necessarily seem to include a scaling back of the peacebuilding duties assigned to operations that are approved.

"Liberal peacebuilding" became the trend in peace operations following the advent of peacebuilding. Liberal peacebuilding is a term that describes the peacekeepers' activities in promoting democracy and free-market economic policies in post-war environments. These require more involvement from the international community rather than a scaling back of duties.

The liberalist approach to peacebuilding has come under increased critique that it does more harm than good. Some of the specific critiques are that (a) democratization and marketization are unlikely to succeed (citing Iraq and Afghanistan a decade after the intervention) and that conflicts should be left to burn out and (b) liberal peacebuilding amounts to the imposition of Western/imperialist values reminiscent of colonialism and "cultural racism." Nevertheless, Paris (2010) argues that such critiques make several mistakes, such as conflating the US-led invasions in Iraq and Afghanistan with liberal peacebuilding operations led by international organizations and mischaracterizing the record of peacebuilding.

Explanations for the Development of Peacebuilding

The development of peace operations was the outcome of an evolutionary process, with many precedents to be found in prior operations. Nevertheless, peacebuilding did not come to full fruition until the 1990s, raising the questions of why such operations emerged then and with such frequency. There are several explanations, all of which are explicitly or implicitly related.[5]

The most common explanation for the emergence of peacebuilding is a supply-side story focused on the end of the Cold War, conventionally designated as occurring around 1989 (although it is better understood as a process rather than a fixed point). As noted in the historical narrative above and the description of historical trends below, peace operations changed dramatically after this time. The end of the Cold War is said to be associated with superpower retrenchment in providing aid to other states and a reluctance to intervene in civil conflicts; the resulting vacuum paved the way for more expansive peace operations that could address the conflicts "dumped" on them by the superpowers. The thawing of the superpower rivalry also broke the stalemate in the UN Security Council that had historically limited peace operations in both number and scope.

The end of the Cold War seems better able to explain the dramatic increase in the number of peace operations than it does the expansion of their duties. There was greater willingness on the part of the permanent members of the Security Council, and indeed the international community of states as a whole, to let the United Nations (and increasingly other international organizations) handle conflicts. Nevertheless, the new functions assigned to peace operations were not those carried out by the superpowers in the past, nor were aid programs provided by those leading powers designed to address similar problems. The end of the Cold War provided the opportunity to conduct more operations, but this particular change in the international system does not necessarily account for the expansion of tasks in those operations.

A second explanation focuses on the demand side of the equation – namely, that peacebuilding arises because most of the threats to international peace and security in the 1990s and beyond were civil conflicts, including those within failed states. There is clear empirical evidence that civil conflicts have become more common than interstate ones (Hewitt, Wilkenfeld, and Gurr 2008), and failed or disrupted states are indeed recent phenomena. Yet the frequency of peace operations conducted by the UN, regional organizations, and other actors is not commensurate with the increase in the number of civil conflicts. Balas, Owsiak, and Diehl (2012) determined that civil conflicts increased by 11 to 38 percent from the Cold War period to the post-Cold War era, but the rate of UN intervention increase exceeds 450 percent for the same period. These findings do not support the argument that an increase in civil conflicts led to a proportional increase in peacebuilding operations. Nonetheless, their research does reveal that the rate of peace operations mirrors more closely the number of conflicts that ended with negotiated agreements, which often included requests for peacebuilding assistance. Thus, there may be some merit for the demand-side explanation, but focused on negotiated agreements rather than on the increase in civil conflicts alone. Still, the choice of actions may be better accounted for by other explanations.

Scholars have also emphasized two, largely interrelated explanations, based on normative change and globalization, respectively, to account for the rise of peacebuilding. The normative change argument has several variants. Balas, Owsiak, and Diehl (2012) argue that a substantial shift in three related norms (sovereignty, humanitarian intervention, and democratization) could be responsible for a shift toward peacebuilding. In the post-Cold War era, there has been a normative transformation to greater concern for the individual, human rights, and government legitimacy and a corresponding decline in the strength of state sovereignty. Thus, it is easier to overrule the omnipotence of sovereignty and deploy peacekeepers.

Second, a norm of humanitarian intervention has been established, and the international community has an obligation (albeit not necessarily a legal one) to take action to redress wrongdoing (Weiss 2012). In this context, peacebuilding activities become a logical extension of military interventions, which alone cannot solve the problems encountered. This approach also recognizes global democratization as a key element but puts more emphasis on international humanitarian norms.

Third, as noted in the previous section, the ideology of liberalism is the guiding force behind peacebuilding operations (Paris 2004). The promotion of democracy and open markets represents attempts to transform states such that they will become peaceful and productive members of the international community. This is consistent with the notion of peacebuilding as a set of activities for peaceful conflict management. A consensus on liberalism, at least in the West, came about only with the end of the Cold War. Yet it is highly unlikely that peacebuilding will cease to exist even if it did not promote liberal policies as its central focus.

Jakobsen (2002) tries to make an integrative argument, using globalization as the central explanation for the rise of peacebuilding; he contends that globalizing forces are the significant and intervening variable connecting the end of the Cold War with the transformation of peace operations. Although somewhat vague on what he means by globalization, he argues that it has produced the normative changes in the areas of human rights and democracy that other scholars cite. Yet he also argues that economic liberalism in the international system, and accompanying conditionality in economic aid programs, has created greater conflict and state failure in underdeveloped states. In addition, globalization has increased media coverage of human suffering and thereby pressures for intervention and actions to deal with such problems.

"Robust" Peacekeeping and the Quest for Order

With some difficult missions, it became apparent that the lack of security, evidenced by the breakdown of law and order, seriously complicated the ability of the peace operations to achieve their longer-term goals. Economic development, human rights protection, and reconciliation are jeopardized when there is still widespread criminal activity, terrorism, and other acts of violence. With more peace operations deployed to civil war contexts and more peacebuilding tasks assigned, the problem of order became acute. Much as traditional peacekeeping operations evolved into peacebuilding, so too did peacebuilding operations adapt to meet the need for order. "Security first" became the priority for some missions, and two notable adaptations have been made for some post-Cold War operations: the incorporation of international civilian police (CIVPOL) and "robust" peacekeeping.

International civilian police have become integrated into peace operations in response to the breakdown of law and order in host countries that lack an indigenous capacity to address the problem. CIVPOL personnel are typically drawn from national police forces, such as the Australian Federal Police, and are tasked with several functions. Initially in the early post-Cold War era, CIVPOL units performed limited roles (Hartz 1999). They monitored the performance of local security forces, reported serious incidents to authorities, and provided advice and training to the police of the host government. In some cases, this more passive role was inadequate, as the local government, or in the case of failed states the absence of local government, could not maintain order with indigenous capacity. Thus, CIVPOL's mandate was expanded to allow units full authority to make arrests and use deadly force if necessary – something that was first permitted in Kosovo. CIVPOL form one component of a broader strategy to restore or create a functioning criminal justice system that includes functioning courts. In 2013, over 15 percent of the personnel deployed in UN peace operations were CIVPOL, illustrating the increasingly important role that these individuals play in contemporary missions.

Certain conflicts have not afforded peacebuilding operations the opportunity to maintain order, either because such order doesn't exist, or because it is subject to dramatic interruption by armed violence that cannot be suppressed by police authority. The widespread violence in Sierra Leone and Afghanistan is illustrative. In those circumstances, a different peacekeeping strategy is essential; as suggested by Jean-Marie

Guéhenno, Under-Secretary-General for Peacekeeping Operations at the UN: "when you do deploy, you need to be sufficiently strong so that if parties on the margin try to use violence to undermine the process, you can hit them hard" (Guéhenno 2006:18).

Robust peacekeeping moves peace operations further toward the coercive end of the use-of-force scale. Such operations involve a larger number of troops than standard operations, and those troops have greater military capability, with weaponry well beyond the traditional rifle or side arms carried by traditional peacekeepers. Rules of engagement are also more permissive, allowing soldiers to initiate the use of force if necessary to carry out their duties, but they will be unable to stop the renewal of warfare if the primary protagonists are determined to start fighting again. Rather, robust peacekeepers are focused on preventing spoilers (marginalized groups, terrorists, etc.) from using violence to undermine the peace process. Peacekeepers might also be charged with deterring or stopping massacres committed against civilian populations – tragedies that occurred as conventional peacekeepers stood by in Rwanda and Bosnia.

The Holy Trinity Revisited

As noted above, traditional peacekeeping was designed according to the holy trinity of host-state consent, impartiality, and minimum use of force. As peace operations evolved, so too did these components. Originally, host-state consent was absolute: peacekeeping operations were not deployed, and did not remain, without the consent of the state on whose territory they were located. This was both a political and an international legal principle. Yet, as peace operations changed, sovereignty was less of a barrier (see a full discussion in chapter 5). Peace operations were deployed in circumstances in which host-state consent was wholly absent (e.g., Kosovo, where the sovereign former Yugoslavia was the target of NATO military action), as well as in failed states (e.g., Somalia) in which consent was impossible.

Impartiality also underwent some significant revision. Originally, this meant that peacekeepers would not favor any party in the conflict, and that their deployment would present no advantage or disadvantage militarily to any side in a conflict. More recently, peace operations have supported government forces over rebel groups (e.g., ISAF in Afghanistan) or democratic forces against the *de facto* government (e.g., Operation Uphold Democracy in Haiti). Missions now may explicitly or implicitly support one side in a conflict. Thus, some peace operations have moved from being third parties in a conflict to being one of the primary parties. The dilemma that the peacekeepers may face in some operations, however, is in favoring one side to facilitate a political transition while trying to maintain impartiality in ensuring humanitarian goals (Eide et al. 2005).

Perhaps the biggest change in the holy trinity has been with respect to the use of force. Traditional peacekeeping permitted military actions only in self-defense. Subsequent peacekeeping and peacebuilding operations with expanded missions, such as the protection of civilian populations, necessitated greater military capability and looser rules of engagement. When we reach robust peacekeeping operations, the distinctions with respect to regular military operations are harder to discern. There is still the principle that only necessary force should be used, but such necessary force now encompasses offensive tactics and considerable firepower, including air strikes in some cases. Although all peace operations have not abandoned the original three principles, there is now considerably more variation along the three dimensions than ever before.

Peacekeeping Doctrine and Related Concerns

The United Nations
In 2000, the United Nations began a major reform process of its peace operations. The first step in this process was the so-called Brahimi Report, which recommended a number of changes. Among these recommendations were

- increasing conflict prevention activities
- establishing clear, credible, and achievable mandates
- facilitating faster deployments (in between thirty and ninety days, depending on the complexity of the peace operation)
- establishing standby forces
- creating general guidelines for disarmament, demobilization, and reintegration) of military forces (DDR)
- integrating civilian police and the rule of law in peace operations
- developing quick impact projects.

Ten years later, a review of the Brahimi recommendations indicates that the Department of Peacekeeping Operations has been strengthened, and a new Department of Field Support was created in 2007 to deal with the logistical issues of fast deployments of peacekeepers in difficult environments. Integrated missions employing a mix of civilian, police, and military capabilities have become the norm. Rule of law and quick impact projects are integral to the peacebuilding activities performed by the peacekeepers. More was required, and the change in peacekeeping doctrine and activities that started with the Brahimi Report was continued in two other documents, the Capstone Doctrine (United Nations 2008) and the New Horizon Report (United Nations 2009b).

The Capstone Doctrine clarified that UN peacekeepers should deal with stabilization and the early stages of peace consolidation, but not with long-term recovery and development.

The long-term aspects are to be left to organizations that are better suited for these roles, such as the World Bank, the International Monetary Fund, other agencies within the UN system, and NGOs. Whenever needed, however, multidimensional peace operations have to get involved in peacebuilding activities that, in addition to stabilizing the conflict and consolidating peace, contribute to recovery and development. Some of these recommended activities repeat those from the Brahimi Report: disarmament, demobilization and reintegration (DDR) of combatants, security sector reform (SSR) and other rule of law-related activities, protection and promotion of human rights, and support for the restoration of state authority. The doctrine recognizes that peacekeeping is just one tool in the third-party intervention toolbox of the United Nations and that this tool is designed to work best for some activities, but not for others.

The factors associated with successful peace operations, the relationship with regional organizations, and the conceptual differences between peace enforcement and robust peacekeeping are three other areas in which the Capstone Doctrine made significant contributions to the reform process. Legitimacy, credibility, and local ownership are three factors identified as essential for the success of a peace operation. Legitimacy is conferred by the mandate derived from the international community through the Security Council. Yet, the peacekeepers' perceived legitimacy on the ground is related more to their behavior and interactions with the local community than by a UN resolution. In order to be a credible presence, peacekeepers should deploy fast, with adequate resources and political will, and be able to respond positively to the pressing needs of the local population. Finally, local ownership of the peace process is required in order to build sustainable peace that will eventually allow the peacekeepers to exit the conflict. Partnerships with local communities and national institutions are judged to be essential for establishing sustainable local ownership.

In 2009, the United Nations released the third major document in the reform process of peace operations, a peace-keeping partnership agenda about the purpose, actions, and the future of peace operations. The New Horizon Report, as this partnership agenda became known, aimed to revitalize the cooperation between the different stakeholders within the United Nations, troop-contributing countries, and other agencies deployed in the field by setting "achievable immediate, medium and long term goals – to help configure UN peace-keeping to meet the challenges of today and tomorrow." The partnership aims to clarify the mandates, objectives, and strategies of the peace operations, to improve the communication involving all relevant stakeholders and local communities, and to create informal, mission-specific coalitions at the headquarters to maintain political support for the missions.

The partnership in action suggests faster deployment and a sequenced roll-out of the deployment in order to respond more quickly to immediate priorities, including the protection of civilians. It also suggests clarifying the concept of "robust peacekeeping" and setting some immediate peacebuilding priorities that should support basic safety and security, political processes, provision of basic services, restoring core government functions, and economic revitalization. The partnership for the future recommends cooperation with regional organizations active in the field by pooling resources and also extending troops' rotation cycles beyond six-month periods in order to maintain experienced personnel for a longer period of time. This new document reiterates some of the recommendations from the Brahimi Report (faster deployment, improved conceptual clarity, and realistic mandates) and highlights ways for improving peace operations in the short and medium term.

European Union
The European Union is the only other international organization that has made major contributions to peacekeeping doctrine. Even though we agree that the European Union does not have yet a clearly set peacekeeping doctrine (Tardy 2006), the predominantly civilian aspect of its peace operations, with their emphasis on peacebuilding and conflict prevention activities, and its development of rapid reaction forces are major contributions to the way peacekeeping is conducted in the twenty-first century.

The European Union is a newcomer to peace operations, having deployed peacekeepers only since 2003. Since then, however, it has become a major actor in peace operations, as it has deployed the second largest number of peace operations after the United Nations (a total of twenty-eight as of January 2013). The Lisbon Treaty updated the circumstances under which the EU can deploy peace operations to take in "joint disarmament operations, humanitarian and rescue tasks, military advice and assistance tasks, conflict prevention and peace-keeping tasks, tasks of combat forces in crisis management, including peace-making and post-conflict stabilisation" (Article 28B.1).

The European Union deploys predominantly civilian crisis management missions that tackle the core issues of the conflict through peacebuilding activities. Nineteen civilian crisis management missions have been deployed (police missions – EUPOL Proxima in FYR Macedonia; rule of law missions – EUJUST LEX in Iraq; civilian administration missions – EULEX Kosovo; border assistance missions – EUBAM Rafah between Israel and the Palestinian Authority; and security sector reform missions – EU SSR in Guinea-Bissau). The military-based peace operations are a minority (nine out of twenty-eight) and involve small numbers of troops (EUFOR Concordia in FYR Macedonia had 320 troops authorized and

150 actually deployed) or are deployed for limited periods of time (Operation Artemis in the Democratic Republic of the Congo was deployed for three months).

The United Nations and other international organizations might learn from the European Union regarding the deployment of rapid reaction and standby forces for peace operations. The development of rapid reaction forces, a goal of the Helsinki European Council (1999), allows the EU to deploy 60,000 troops within sixty days to the field, for one year. The EU Battle groups are standing battalion-size multinational military units (1,500 soldiers) ready to be deployed in a crisis. Every six months, military units from two or three EU member states form a battle group and could be deployed within thirty days as needed. The EU Gendarmerie Force is formed from the militarized police units of six member states and has approximately 800 to 900 members that could deploy within thirty days to deal with crises.

Human Security, the Responsibility to Protect (R2P), and the Protection of Civilians

Human security, the responsibility to protect (R2P), and the protection of civilians are three intellectually related concepts that overlap, leading to confusion and controversy in the context of peace operations. First, human security could be thought of as the overarching goal that identifies global problems from the perspective of the individual, rather than the state, and it includes hunger, disease, inequality, violence, disasters, and poverty. Human security applies all the time, not only in times of war. It also applies everywhere, in the developed as well as the developing world. Sovereignty and the role of state institutions are essential in achieving human security. Second, the responsibility to protect (R2P) places the responsibility to ensure the safety of its population on each individual member state. In cases when states are not able or not willing to protect their population from "genocide, war crimes, ethnic cleansing and crimes against humanity," however, the international community has a responsibility to intervene and protect the people. R2P is narrower than human security, confined to high-intensity conflicts. Sovereignty could be infringed upon in the name of R2P. Finally, protection of civilians finds its roots in international humanitarian law. Peacekeepers are required to protect civilians from imminent threat of physical violence. Actions in the name of protection of civilians do not infringe upon the sovereignty of states and often occur in post-conflict environments when the intensity of violence is reduced. Protection of civilians is incorporated within the larger concept of human security and could be an activity required under the high-intensity conflicts covered by R2P, but it is also applied in less intense conflicts.

The role of peace operations in achieving human security is still unclear almost two decades after the concept joined the peace, security, and development agenda of the international community in the early 2000s. What is the relationship between peace operations and human security? For a start, the concept of "human security" is barely mentioned in United Nations peacekeeping documents, and the same goes for peace operations concepts in the human security literature. The conceptual links are not fully developed yet. But if we analyze the mandates of peace operations and the key human security clusters of activities in the aftermath of violent conflict (public safety, humanitarian relief, rehabilitation and reconstruction, reconciliation and coexistence, and governance and empowerment), we observe that peacebuilding operations contain elements of human security.

The mandates of many peace operations require peacekeepers to conduct activities on human security issues of public safety, humanitarian relief, rehabilitation and reconstruction, and governance and empowerment. For public safety, peacekeepers might be asked to control armed groups, protect civilians (especially women and children), and build and provide training for national security institutions (police, military; integrate and dissolve non-state military actors). For humanitarian relief, peacekeepers could be tasked with improving their cooperation with humanitarian and development aid agencies in order to protect the delivery of food and medicine to internally displaced persons (IDPs) and refugees. For rehabilitation and reconstruction, the peacekeepers started developing community projects to fix roads, build schools, provide electricity, and (re-)establish a market economy. For governance and empowerment, peacekeepers can facilitate the promotion of democratization, human rights, civil society participation, and the rule of law at both the national and local levels. For reconciliation and coexistence, peacebuilding operations might cooperate with local communities to bring people to justice and to set up truth and reconciliation committees in order to promote forgiveness and to encourage community-based coexistence projects. Thus, even though, at a conceptual level, peace operations and human security seem separate, at an activities level we notice how human security goals have found their space in peace operations mandates, especially for peacebuilding operations.

The protection of civilians is one of the human security aspects that has received specific attention from the United Nations peacekeepers since 1999, when the Security Council tasked peacekeepers with protecting civilians in new missions in Sierra Leone (UNAMSIL) and East Timor (INTERFET and UNTAET) respectively. Nevertheless, a 2009 study showed that there is still a long way to go from mandate to implementation in the area of protection of civilians: "the UN Secretariat, troop- and police-contributing countries, host states, humanitarian actors, human rights professionals, and the missions themselves continue to struggle over what it means for a peacekeeping operation to protect civilians, in definition and in practice" (Holt, Taylor, and Kelly 2009: 4). The same study reports that "the most common association of the concept [protection of civilians] in the context of peacekeeping centered on the protection of civilians from imminent threat of physical violence" (ibid.: 5) The 2012 *Human Security Report* (Human Security Report Project 2012) wonders if the protection of civilians by peacekeepers is an "impossible mandate," given their scarce resources and unclear policy guidelines. Goetz (2008: 4) thinks that "stopping wartime sexual violence amounts to a 'doubly impossible'" mandate for UN peacekeepers, given that sometimes a small number of peacekeepers are responsible for the sexual violence themselves.

Notwithstanding these critiques about the ability of peacekeepers to protect civilians, there have been some significant improvements since 2009. Resolution 1894 (2009) reaffirmed the "important role peacekeeping operations play for the protection of civilians" and requested comprehensive operational guidance for implementing this mandate. As of 2012, eight out of the sixteen UN peace operations had a protection of civilians mandate, and three (MONUSCO, UNOCI, and UNAMID) have implemented comprehensive protection of civilians strategies. In addition, the UN Secretariat developed a series of training modules for peacekeepers on the protection of civilians and created the position of "Protection of Civilians Coordination Officer" within the Department of Peacekeeping Operations. These changes suggest that human security in the form of protection of civilians is becoming a major component of the peacekeepers' mandate.

Humanitarian relief, rehabilitation and reconstruction, governance and empowerment, and reconciliation and coexistence are human security clusters that have also been mainstreamed throughout peace operations. Peacekeepers with the UNAMID operation often provide security to humanitarian convoys in Darfur, Sudan, and sometimes even transport relief items such as blankets, mattresses, and mosquito nets. Community violence reduction programs have become a component of most peace operations deployed by the United Nations, and include activities such as cleaning canals, improving sanitation, building schools, and fixing roads, as happened in Haiti (MINUSTAH) or in the DR Congo (MONUC). These programs are also ways to employ young people (either previously part of rebel groups or potential recruits for rebel groups) and jump-start the local economy. Truth and reconciliation commissions have been set up in peacebuilding missions, as in UNAMSIL in Sierra Leone. The peacekeepers there trained the local population on human rights issues, were instrumental in setting up the Special Court for Sierra Leone, and assisted the government in establishing a truth and reconciliation commission. Finally, the area in which the peace operations have done the most is in governance and empowerment. Since 1989, new peace operations have organized and supervised elections, conducted democratization activities, promoted the rule of law, and trained local bureaucrats, civil society, and local media in places such as Namibia, Cambodia, El Salvador, Bosnia, Kosovo, and the DR Congo.

Patterns in Peace Operations

In the event of a fire, fire-fighters are supposed to respond to blazes whenever and wherever they take place. In theory, international or regional agencies should intervene in all serious conflicts and attempt to manage or resolve them. In practice, this is far from the case. Thus, there is not a perfect correlation between the list of violent conflicts and the list of peace operations. First, the deployment of a peace operation is only one option available, and the international community may choose more coercive or more likely diplomatic alternatives instead. Indeed, these may be superior options given the kind of conflict and other aspects of the situation at hand. Still, peace operations are not always deployed even when they are arguably well suited to dealing with a conflict. This section of the chapter looks at the general factors that determine where peacekeepers are deployed and how long those deployments last; then various patterns of peace operation deployment over space and time are described.

Where Do Peacekeepers Go?

Although peacekeepers are not sent to all serious conflicts, neither is it the case that they are sent to a random set.[6] This concern was ignored for years in peacekeeping research, and only a few studies have inquired about the conditions for peacekeeping deployment.

Several scholars (Gibbs 1997; Oudraat 1996) have asserted that the national interests of the major power states determine where peacekeepers are sent.[7] Yet there have been few systematic studies that test such assertions. Mullenbach (2005) argues that international-level factors, rather than those related to the conflict itself, best account for decisions to create peace operations. Specifically, he notes that the authorization of a peace operation is less likely when the target state has an alliance with a major power or is a major power itself. Of course, this misses the significant number of peace operations deployed to various elements of the superpower proxy wars between Israel and her Arab neighbours (e.g., UNDOF) as well as to certain civil wars in Africa, such as in Angola (UNAVEM I). In contrast, peace missions are more likely when there was prior involvement by the UN or a regional organization. This suggests that peace operations are not usually the first option selected, but follow either some progress or possibly some failure on the diplomatic front.

Most scholars focus on conditions associated with a conflict to explain mission onset. Gilligan and Stedman (2003) examine post-Cold War civil conflicts and conclude that peace operations are more likely to be deployed in high-severity and protracted conflicts. On the one hand, this is encouraging, in that the international community is taking action against the biggest threats to international peace and security. On the other hand, it suggests that peace operations will have difficulty succeeding, as they are deployed to contexts with the least prospects for success (see chapter 4). The authors also find that operations are less likely in states with large government armies, reflecting some respect for state sovereignty or recognition that a small peace force is unlikely to compel large entities to change their behavior.

The Gilligan and Stedman study is perhaps most important for what the authors did not find, dispelling many myths about peace operations. There was no evidence that missions were more likely in secessionist conflicts, non-democracies, former colonies of UN Security Council members, or states with high primary commodity exports. Each of those factors was thought to provide incentives for third parties, especially leading states, to intervene in weaker states.

Similarly, Fortna (2004a) identifies a number of factors not associated with peacekeeping operations, including identity conflicts, among others. Yet, she makes an important distinction between different kinds of missions (consent- vs. enforcement-based), the organizing agencies of the operations (UN vs. other), and temporal patterns (Cold War vs. post-Cold War). Controlling for these distinctions, Fortna finds that various factors that have clear or no effects in the aggregate (e.g., government army size, war severity, and democracy) may have context-specific impacts, although the relationships uncovered are not especially strong. Nevertheless, she still concludes that consent-based peacekeeping does tend to be involved in the most difficult cases.

How Long Do They Stay?
Continuing with the fire-fighting analogy, ideally peacekeepers should stay deployed until they are no longer needed. At the same time, there are political and financial pressures, especially from contributing states, to withdraw forces as soon as possible. In practice, peace operations have varied tremendously in terms of how long they last. The mean length of a peace operation is 5.69 years, ranging from just a few months (EU Operation Artemis in the DR Congo) to more than sixty-five years (UNTSO in the Middle East).[8]

Over time, the duration of peace missions has become shorter; most obviously, the longest operations were those first deployed during the Cold War period, and these include several operations still in existence today (e.g., UNFICYP; UNIFIL). Yet this trend is not merely a function of older operations having been "born" earlier. Operations in civil wars, which are more common in recent times, have traditionally been shorter than those deployed to interstate conflicts. In addition, post-Cold War peacekeeping has tended to be characterized by multiple and consecutive operations, each of which is of limited duration, sent to the same conflict, rather than by a single operation that stays in place for an extended time; multiple operations sent to Haiti and the former Yugoslavia exhibit this characteristic.

Few would argue that peace operations stay as long as they are needed, and indeed most casual observers believe that peacekeepers leave too soon. Wright and Greig (2012) examined only UN operations in civil conflicts, but nonetheless provide some of the only evidence and explanations on the duration of peace operations. They define peace operations as "durable" if the operation stays in place until the conflict is terminated. Among those operations that have ended, slightly less than 50 percent meet this standard. What accounts for this suboptimal outcome? The authors cite three major factors as affecting the durability of peace operations. One is that peace operations that facilitate some traction toward peace – that is, promote the other conditions for conflict management and resolution – are more likely to stay until the end; in contrast, when circumstances on the ground or at the negotiating table are going poorly, UN operations tend to leave prematurely. Yet conditions on the ground are not the only determinant of operation duration – political decisions by member states matter as well. When member states find that the costs and risks of the operation diminish, and when they are willing to increase the operational capacity of the mission, the operation tends to "stay the course."

An Overview of Peace Operations

As noted in the previous chapter, there are various military activities that are labeled as "peacekeeping" or "peace operations," and any list of such operations that purports to be comprehensive is subject to some debate over what cases should or should not be included. For analysis of patterns over time and space, we have chosen to rely on the list of operations compiled by the Henry Stimson Center, covering the period 1948–2006 and extended by Balas (2011b); a full list of the operations and their beginning and ending dates is given in the appendix.[9] Although this list contains some cases (e.g., Indian actions in Sri Lanka) that border on standard military interventions and some cases (e.g., EUCAP Sahel Niger) that barely qualify as civilian peacebuilding, the collection is perhaps the most recent and definitive available, covering UN, regional organization, and multinational missions. According to this list, there have been 188 peace operations over the

Table 2.1 Peace operations by decade			
Decade	Initiated	Ended	Ongoing
1940s	2	0	2
1950s	4	3	3
1960s	7	7	3
1970s	7	2	8
1980s	12	8	12
1990s	83	52	43
2000s	63	52	54
2010s	10	11	53
Total	188	135	53

period studied, fifty-three of which were still in existence at the beginning of 2013. Yet these operations are hardly distributed equally along a series of different dimensions.

Temporal Patterns
The number of new peace operation initiations and the number of ongoing operations are set out in table 2.1. Peace operations were relatively few during the Cold War period, with barely more than one new operation authorized every two years. The 1980s, particularly the last few years of the decade, signal a change in frequency, with more than one new operation every year. An explosion in peace operations occurs in the 1990s, with eight new operations per year. The rate of initiation then slows somewhat after 2000, with approximately six new operations every year, a rate still well above the historic average.

Another measure of peace operation frequency over time is the number of ongoing operations. At the end of 2012, there were still fifty-three peace operations in place, more than one-fourth of all those ever authorized, as indicated in figure 2.1), this represents an all-time high. Several of these opera-

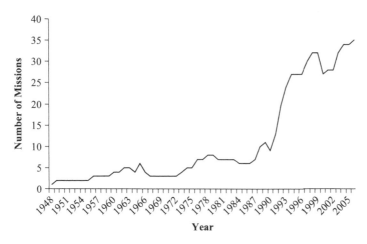

Figure 2.1 Ongoing peace operations (by year)

tions are long-standing operations from the Cold War period, such as UNTSO in the Middle East and UNFICYP in Cyprus. Others are of more recent vintage, such as UNMIL in Liberia and RAMSI in the Solomon Islands.

The international community is hypothesized to have a "carrying capacity" for peace operations; that is, there are limited resources and diplomatic attention that can be devoted to peace operations at any given juncture (see fuller discussion in chapter 5). Viewed from this perspective, that capacity has increased over time. Still, one might surmise that the number, cost, and effectiveness of existing operations influence the likelihood of future decisions to deploy operations. There is a fatigue effect that comes from the conduct of peace operations, especially when problems arise with current operations. The slight decline in the rate of new operations after 2000 might also be attributable to the scope of existing commitments. The large number of ongoing operations and the large number of troops and civilian personnel committed to those operations (the UN alone had more than 110,000

Table 2.2 Total peace operations by region	
Region	Number of operations
Central and South Asia	11
Europe	46
Latin America and the Caribbean	19
Middle East and North Africa	24
Pacific	5
Southeast Asia	9
Sub-Saharan Africa	74

personnel deployed, with more committed, at the end of 2012; see United Nations 2012) may in part be responsible for the reluctance of the UN and regional organizations to commit themselves to new ventures.

Geographic Patterns
Peace operations have also varied significantly by region of deployment, as indicated in table 2.2. Sub-Saharan Africa has had almost twice as many operations (seventy-four) as any other region, with most of these coming since 1990. An example is the AMIB operation in Burundi. Much of this is no doubt a function of the increase in conflict "demand" in that region, but the greater willingness and capability of regional organizations to conduct operations must be part of the explanation as well (five different African institutions deployed peace operations on the continent). Throughout the Cold War, Europe was excluded from all but one peace operation (UNFICYP in Cyprus), but the end of the Cold War opened up not only the possibility for peace operations but also long-standing tensions that would generate the need for such operations. Conflict in the Balkans led to no fewer than thirty-one operations by global and regional organizations. Similarly, the territory of the former Soviet Union was

an area outside the realm of peacekeepers. Since the breakup of the Soviet Union, however, there have been peace operations sent to a number of former client territories, including, for example, Georgia (UNOMIG, CPKF, and an OSCE mission respectively). The Western hemisphere, traditionally the sphere of influence of the United States, has seen an increase in peace operations since the end of the Cold War as well.

The Middle East is perhaps the only region that has consistently been the site of violent conflicts and peace operations designed to mitigate them. The Southeast and Northeast Asian regions are perhaps the ones most underserved by peace operations relative to other geographic areas and conflict frequency therein. Except for the peace operations in East Timor and Aceh, Southeast Asia has not seen new peace operations since Cambodia in the early 1990s. Northeast Asia has had no peace operations. Neither area has well-developed regional organizations (Northeast Asia has none) to carry out peace operation activities, but the UN has also been largely absent from these areas as well.

Conflict Patterns
Early in their history, peace operations were confined largely to conflicts between states. Thus, the first observation missions were sent to the Arab–Israeli (UNTSO) and Indian–Pakistani (UNMOGIP) rivalries respectively. This pattern continued through the 1970s, with internal issues drawing attention only as they intersected with decolonization concerns, as was the case in the Western New Guinea (UNTEA/UNSF) and the Congo (ONUC).

As mentioned above, an explosion of peace operations into conflicts that have an exclusive or significant internal conflict component occurred in the 1990s. Since then, such operations have constituted almost 90 percent of new ventures, whereas previously they were a minority. Since 2000, the only operation sent to a purely interstate conflict was the one deployed following the Ethiopian–Eritrean War (UNMEE); although this was a war between two states, its origins are found in the internal secessionist conflict less than a decade earlier that resulted in Eritrean independence.

What accounts for this sudden shift in the kinds of conflict to which peace operations are deployed? There are perhaps two primary explanations. First is the increase in civil wars during this period. The number of civil conflicts proliferated with the end of the Cold War, and there was a decline in the number of interstate wars, at least for the decade of the 1990s. Equally important was the scope and intensity of those wars. Civil conflicts increasingly had "negative externalities" or spillover effects on neighboring states, threatening international peace and security as well as providing impetus for the international community to act; such effects included refugee flows, cross-border fighting, and even genocide. Second, there was a normative shift by the international community in its view of state sovereignty and external intervention. Previously, state sovereignty was considered almost absolute; what occurred within the borders of states was considered largely beyond the domain of other states. With the development of human rights and other concerns, international norms no longer supported the "hard shell" of state sovereignty and began to recognize that the international community had legitimate interests in what was the domestic jurisdiction of states. This shift has had profound consequences in a number of areas (e.g., human rights, environmental protection), but it also legitimized the use of peace operations in internal conflicts. For example, six different peace operations have been deployed to quell internal troubles in Haiti, whereas previously these would have attracted only military intervention by regional powers or no action at all. Third, the number of civil wars that ended with negotiated agreements requesting the

Table 2.3 Total peace operations by agency type	
Agency	Operations
United Nations	76
United Nations/regional organization	2
Regional	91
Multinational	19

deployment of peacekeepers increased significantly. These demands were cautiously answered by the United Nations, initially, and by other regional organizations, soon thereafter, thus multiplying the number of deployments in civil conflicts.

Organizational Patterns
Finally, there has been a notable change in the primary organizing agencies for peace operations over time. The aggregate figures are given in table 2.3, with the UN conducting about 40 percent of all operations. The frequency of UN intervention in the form of peace operations has not necessarily changed; that organization has continued its historical role of deploying more new operations than other agencies. Rather, the major change has been the increasing role of regional organizations and multinational peace missions; they have not replaced UN operations (there is no evidence of "dumping"; see Wallensteen and Heldt 2008) but have filled in the gaps left by the global organization. Early regional efforts were relatively uncommon and often indistinguishable from actions by leading states, such as Syria in Lebanon. Later, however, more collective actions, rather than the mere authorization of action by leading states, became the norm, illustrated by the AMIS mission in Sudan initiated by the African Union in 2004. As of 2012, thirteen different regional organizations had deployed at least one peace operation (EU, OSCE, AU, NATO, OAS, ECOWAS, LAS, CIS, Commonwealth, SADC, ECCAS,

PIF, CEMAC). A new model of hybrid peace operations between the UN and a regional organization (OAS, AU) has been initiated (this is discussed in more detail in chapter 3), and multinational groupings have also become more prominent, albeit with one state often taking a leading role in those efforts (e.g., Australian efforts in East Timor, INTERFET).

The increasing role of regional organizations and multinational groupings is more than cosmetic. There are significant implications for the organization, supply, and financing of operations. These issues are addressed in detail in the next chapter.

CHAPTER THREE

The Organization of Peace Operations

As illustrated in the previous chapter, peace operations have varied substantially over time, with a proliferation of missions in the post-Cold War era. Peace operations also vary significantly in how they are organized, funded, and supplied. This chapter addresses these issues, with special attention to describing and evaluating alternatives to existing practices.

Agents

The analysis begins with the most basic of concerns: who conducts peace operations? The traditional organizing agency for most missions has been the United Nations, which is still the organization with the most ongoing peace operations; however, there have been notable trends toward the greater involvement of regional organizations and multilateral groupings of states, and even the prospective involvement of private peace operation suppliers.

The United Nations
Since its inception through 2012, the United Nations has authorized and directed seventy-six peace operations. Although the processes of organizing, financing, and conducting peace operations are unique to the context, there are several clear patterns to these missions.

UN peace operations are authorized by the UN Security Council, and as such require support from nine of the fifteen members of the Council and no opposition from the permanent five members. The mandate of the operation is specified in the authorizing resolution. Missions are typically approved for six-month periods, subject to renewal. With a few exceptions, peace operations are reauthorized without much debate or change in mandate.

The implementation of peace operations is the responsibility of the UN Secretary-General, who ultimately reports to the Security Council. Major operations are under the direction of a "Special Representative" appointed by the Secretary-General. Senior military personnel, including the operation commander, are appointed by the Secretary-General and function as UN civil service employees. For example, the force commander for the UN Mission in Ethiopia and Eritrea has been Major-General Mohammed Taisir Masadeh of Jordan.

Behind the actual forces on the ground is the support infrastructure provided by the United Nations. The Department of Peacekeeping Operations (DPKO) provides a variety of services that assist in the conduct of UN peace operations, with an Under-Secretary-General assigned to manage its tasks. Traditionally, this was a very weak unit with few staff and very little advance planning. Problems with this unit were highlighted in the Brahimi Report, the study released in 2000 by a UN blue ribbon panel charged with identifying ways of improving UN peacekeeping.[1] In that report, it was recommended that DPKO increase its staffing, create a "Best Practices Unit," expand planning, establish a pre-mandate financing mechanism for operations, strengthen training programs, and enhance its logistics base in Italy by stockpiling additional equipment. Nevertheless, not all these changes have been implemented, and the organization remains limited by the constraints imposed upon it by its members.

In 2005, The UN created the Peacebuilding Commission (PBC).[2] This is an advisory body composed of thirty-one member countries, most importantly including the permanent members of the Security Council as well as leading troop and financial contributors to UN peace operations. The PBC functions primarily through country-specific committees focused on states in the fourth phase of conflict – that is, following the cessation of hostilities and the signing of a peace accord – and proposes strategies for assisting these states and encouraging stable financing mechanisms. It is assisted by the Peacebuilding Support Office (PBSO), a professional bureaucratic unit that will prepare reports and provide other substantive information and assessments. In addition, the PBC consults with the Working Group on Lessons Learned in order to incorporate evaluative feedback into its planning.

The PBC was originally designed to enhance coordination between different units of the UN and various stakeholders (see Jenkins 2013 for a full discussion of the PBC). In practice, it has often fallen victim to the national interests of its members, especially those who also sit on the Security Council. Rather than unifying peacebuilding efforts, the PBC has tended to fragment them. A number of reforms have been suggested, and it is unclear at this writing which, if any, will be adopted. These include involving the PBS at the stage at which the mandate is developed rather than only in the implementation phase, engaging more with civil society rather than only with UN members and bureaucracy, facilitating reconciliation in post-conflict societies, and implementing better management practices among others (IPI 2013).

The restructuring of the DPKO and the creation of the Peacebuilding Commission did not signal the end of peace operation reform. In early 2007, UN Secretary-General Ban Ki-moon proposed further organizational changes to meet the expansion in the number and scope of UN peace operations. The DPKO is split into two units: a Department of Peace Operations and a Department of Field Support, each with its own Under-Secretary-General. The latter is responsible for the management of field personnel, supply procurement, and all communication technology. Another change is the increased role played by the Department of Political Affairs in establishing political missions with peacebuilding roles that replace the peacekeepers once an operation has ended. Some of these political missions are considered peace operations because of their civilian peacebuilding mandates (UNIPSIL in Sierra Leone was mandated to promote human rights, democratization, and rule of law). As such, these political missions resemble the European Union's civilian peacebuilding operations.

As UN peace operations have expanded their duties beyond truce supervision, other institutional arrangements have been modified accordingly. Other units of the UN, such as the Electoral Assistance Division, have assisted with election supervision. UN personnel and civilian police from member states have helped set up election machinery, have conducted elections, and helped maintain order during political transitions. Sister agencies of the UN, such as the World Bank, have also been involved in reconstruction efforts. Peacebuilding operations require development strategies and aid from international donors, tasks that are inappropriate for peace operation personnel. Furthermore, NGOs have carried out many humanitarian assistance functions in conjunction or in coordination with peace operation personnel. UN peace operations do not necessarily displace organizations and activities already in place in the area of deployment. Indeed, in most cases this would be foolish, as those organizations have the local knowledge, expertise, and extant arrangements to perform certain tasks more efficiently and more effectively.

Regional Organizations

There is considerable variation in the organization, conduct, and frequency of regional peace operations.[3] The most obvious differences are the institutional capacities for conducting such operations, which condition all other aspects of their policy and performance. The ability of regional organizations to play significant roles is determined largely by the authority granted to them by their members. In some cases, no security institution at all exists in a region, foreclosing the possibility of peace operations except by an ad hoc multinational coalition of regional states. For example, the North Asian region has no regional organization to handle conflict management. In other parts of Asia, the institutions are relatively weak. The South Asian Association for Regional Cooperation (SAARC) provides for cooperation only in areas of social and economic issues. By definition, then, it is unable to exercise any significant role in violent regional conflicts, much less mount a peace operation. Other regional organizations, such as the Association of Southeast Asian Nations (ASEAN), are similarly handicapped by limited mandates for security action.

In other regions, the mandates of organizations and the level of institutionalization vary widely. Until recently, the African Union (primarily its predecessor, the Organization of African Unity) was structurally weak, often no more than a forum for a yearly meeting of heads of state on that continent. Much of this may be a backlash against UN involvement in the Congo during the 1960s and a preference for non-intervention of any variety by outside actors. Accordingly, to the extent that the organization was involved in peace activities, it was through ad hoc committees. The AU has expanded its activities to embrace election monitoring and peace operations, including the deployment of forces to Sudan (AMIS).

Several regional organizations have the legal provisions to undertake a variety of different kinds of actions. The

Organization of American States (OAS) has collective security provisions contained in its Charter (Article 28) as well as provisions for other kinds of action, although most of these are directed against extra-regional threats or interstate aggression rather than internal matters. Similarly, the Gulf Cooperation Council and the League of Arab States have collective security provisions at their disposal. Some regional entities also contain conflict management provisions, even if their primary purposes are in the economic realm.

At the other extreme of the continuum is the European region, which has multiple institutions for dealing with security. These have overlapping memberships and complementary roles. Of longest-standing importance is the North Atlantic Treaty Organization, which traditionally handled the duties for collective security and collective defense. At the end of the Cold War its missions were modified, and it now functions as a peacekeeper in Bosnia, Kosovo, and Afghanistan. NATO has available troops, command structures, and other organizational capacity to carry out peace operations and has deployed thirteen peace operations in the Balkans, Iraq, Afghanistan, Libya, and Somalia. One of the first NATO peace operations after it changed its mission in the early 1990s was the Stabilization Force in Bosnia (SFOR).

NATO initially became involved in the Bosnian conflict in 1995 through the Implementation Force (IFOR) in the aftermath of the Dayton peace agreement. IFOR was tasked with implementing the peace and successfully organizing the general elections in September 1996. It had a mandate of only one year, and in December 1996 the Stabilization Force (SFOR) was set up to continue its work and to stabilize the peace in Bosnia. SFOR had a United Nations Chapter VII mandate that allowed its troops to enforce the peace should the need arise. Besides the peace enforcement activities, it was charged with some early elements of peacebuilding – working

---

Box 3.1 SFOR

SFOR was deployed to enforce the peace that came out of the Dayton Agreement and to work with local civil society to promote a climate in which the peace process could move forward.

Headquarters: Sarajevo

Duration: December 1996 – December 2004

Maximum strength: 32,000

Cost: approximately US$205 million total (estimate), not including the payments made directly to their troops by the NATO member states.

---

with local civil society and promoting a climate in which the peace process could move forward. SFOR worked closely with other international organizations to organize regional and general elections, disarm the paramilitary groups, deal with refugees and internally displaced persons (IDPs), promote local law and order, and repair the infrastructure destroyed by many years of war. SFOR, which was completed successfully in 2004, was a typical NATO peace operation, focused on robust peacekeeping and peace enforcement activities conducted mostly by the military, and with very limited elements of civilian peacebuilding.

Regional organizations have different legal and other capacities for peace operations. They also vary significantly in how they conduct such operations. Rather than describe all of the arrangements for every regional organization, we focus specifically on the EU and the AU respectively, the two associations that have been most active of late in peace operations, at least as regards number of operations.[4]

The European Union has become the second largest provider of peace operations after the United Nations, all since 2003. Table 3.1 shows the European Union deploying twenty-seven peace operations, from the Balkans to Central Africa, from the Middle East to Indonesia – more than the combined number of NATO and OAU/AU operations. Whereas NATO

Table 3.1 Specific organizing agencies of peace operations	
Agency	Number of operations
United Nations	76
European Union	27
Multinational peace operations	19
Organization for Security and Cooperation in Europe (OSCE)	14
North Atlantic Treaty Organization (NATO)	13
Organization of African Unity (OAU)/African Union (AU)	13
Organization of American States (OAS)	7
Economic Community of West African States (ECOWAS)	5
Commonwealth of Independent States (CIS)	2
League of Arab States (LAS)	2
Southern African Development Community	2
Commonwealth Secretariat	2
UN/regional hybrid peace operations	2
Economic Community of Central African States (ECCAS)	1
Economic and Monetary Community of Central Africa (CEMAC)	1
Pacific Islands Forum (PIF)	1

and the AU/OAU are focused on the security of Europe and of Africa, respectively, the European Union is the only organization, besides the UN, that has a global reach for its peace operations. Most of these are civilian peacebuilding interventions, with very limited roles, or none at all, for the military. Nevertheless, there have been a few EU military interventions, such as Operation Artemis in Eastern DR Congo or EUFOR Chad/Central African Republic; these interventions resembled UN missions with a substantial peace enforcement component.

The EU initiates (and terminates) peace operations through the Council of the European Union (Council of Ministers) and requires consensus among the EU member states, but

Box 3.2 EULEX

EULEX Kosovo is a civilian peacebuilding operation that was tasked with strengthening the rule of law in Kosovo, establishing a multi-ethnic justice system, a multi-ethnic police force, and a customs service.

Headquarters: Prishtinë/Priština, Kosovo

Duration: From February 2008 (ongoing)

Maximum Strength: 2,250

Cost: US$144 million per year

planning and management of such operations are delegated to several committees or other EU organizations. The Peace and Security Committee (PSC) maintains responsibility for the day-to-day management of the operation in the field. Meeting at the ambassadorial level, the PSC also coordinates the detailed response to a crisis situation and maintains "political control and strategic direction" over all operations. The Secretary-General/High Representative (SG/HR) provides the fundamental administrative support to field operations. In particular, the SG/HR retains the authority (acting on behalf of the President of the Council) to negotiate agreements with third-party states. The EU Special Representative (EUSR) serves as the operation administrative coordinator in the field and retains responsibility for ensuring the coordination of all EU activities within the conflict area, including military, civilian, and diplomatic efforts. The EUSR reports directly to the SG/HR and the PSC. The Military Committee (EUMC – under the PSC) monitors the military activities of the mission, acting through the EU Operations Commander in the field. Composed of the defense ministers (or their representatives) of the member states, this committee links the field with the organization. The European Union Military Staff (EUMS), acting under the direction of the EUMC and of the EU High Representative for Foreign Affairs and Security Policy, is responsible for planning and implementing military operations and civilian operations with a military dimension, too (e.g., EUFOR Althea). The Military Staff is also responsible for setting up an Operations Center that could be activated for joint military–civilian operations. In 2012 this center became operational and is tasked with coordinating the activities of the EU peace operations in the Horn of Africa. The Civilian Planning and Conduct Capability unit (CPCC – under the PSC), established in 2007, is mandated to plan and conduct civilian operations (e.g., EULEX Kosovo) under the political and strategic leadership of the PSC.

Such arrangements are much more highly segmented than those of the UN, while also integrating more activities in different sectors, such as the civilian and military elements. The EU intervention in Bosnia had a few unusual features, because the operation was taken over from one conducted by NATO (SFOR). A process of rehatting commanders and troops occurs quite often when such transfer happens. For example, NATO's Deputy Supreme Allied Commander for Europe served as the EU Operations Commander for this mission. Another example of the EU taking over from another organization was in Kosovo.

The largest and most expansive civilian peacebuilding operation of the European Union is the European Union Rule of Law Mission in Kosovo (EULEX). EULEX took over the police, justice, and civil administration responsibilities of the United Nations' peace operation in Kosovo (UNMIK) in February 2008. The mission was tasked with strengthening the rule of law in Kosovo, establishing a multi-ethnic justice system, a multi-ethnic police force, and a customs service. The EU deployed civilian police, customs officers, prosecutors, and judges to monitor, mentor, and advise their Kosovar colleagues. EULEX worked closely with the Kosovar institutions, trying to implement the recommendations of the UN Capstone Doctrine regarding local ownership of peace operations. It had also some executive powers regarding war crimes, organized crime, high-level corruption, and terrorism.

Peace operations in which the European Union takes over from an initial UN or NATO peace operation has been the dominant model in European peace operations. "In Europe, the tradition has been for the UN and NATO to hand over missions to the EU" (Derblom, Frisell, and Schmidt 2008: 45). Other examples besides Kosovo are the EU taking over from NATO in Macedonia and from the UN in Bosnia.

The AU is a much less developed organization than the EU, and accordingly its method of organizing peace operations more closely resembles the ad hoc arrangements of the UN. The Peace and Security Council (PSC), made up of fifteen elected member states, has the authority to develop and deploy peace missions, although operations are supposed to have the consent of the organization's Assembly. The Chairperson of the Commission (Secretariat) has responsibility for implementation, including troop solicitation and management. For example, the PSC asked the Chairperson to come up with recommendations to enhance the AMIS mission after its initial deployment of a small number of observers was deemed inadequate. Two supplementary bodies, the Military Staff Committee and the Commissioner in Charge of Peace and Security, provide advice and support to peace operations. A Force Commander and a Special Representative complete the key field personnel; for example, Daniel Moenyana of South Africa served as the AMIS Force Commander and Dr Salim Ahmed Salim, a Tanzanian diplomat, was the AU's special representative to Darfur.

The precursor to the African Union, the Organization of African Unity, deployed seven peace operations, primarily observer missions. The African Union deployed six peace operations of its own and a hybrid operation together with the United Nations (UNAMID). The first fully fledged peace operation of the African Union, the African Mission in Burundi (AMIB), was deployed from 2003 to 2004, as demanded by the Arusha Agreement (2000) and the 2002 ceasefire agreement – two negotiated agreements that aimed to end the Burundi civil war started in 1993. The mandate of AMIB was to oversee the implementation of the ceasefire agreement, but also to conduct DDR activities and facilitate the delivery of humanitarian aid to the population, refugees, and internally displaced persons (IDPs). AMIB was able to implement the ceasefire and improve the defense and security situation in approximately 95 percent of the territory of Burundi.

This type of peace operation, in which the regional organization takes the lead and the United Nations deploys a peace operation later, became the model for other peace operations in Africa. In thirteen out of the fifteen African cases in which there is a transfer of peacekeeping responsibilities, the transfer occurs from the regional organization (AU, ECOWAS, CEMAC) to the more experienced and resourceful organizations (UN). "The AU forces can be deployed early in a conflict situation and the UN only engages after there is an overarching peace agreement in place" (Derblom, Frisell, and Schmidt 2008: 45).

Multinational and Unilateral Operations
Multinational peace operations are those conducted by more than one country and not under the auspices of any international organization. These are ad hoc missions that may arise because the United Nations and regional organizations cannot agree on authorizing a mission and/or the disputants reject a peace operation carried out by those institutions. For example, the Multinational Force and Observers (MFO), an eleven-nation consortium and a by-product of the Camp David peace process, have been deployed between Israel and

Egypt since the early 1980s, largely because Israel rejected any further UN operations there.

Multinational missions use standard national military institutions to carry out the operations. The exact organizational scheme and rules of engagement must be negotiated for each mission. Operations such as the MFO are well integrated and are composed of states with extensive experience of cooperating with one another. In contrast, other operations may be nothing more than the sum of their national parts, with those component units having separate responsibilities and rules of engagement. For example, the Multinational Force (MNF) deployed in Beirut in 1982–4 was made up of four national units (the US, the UK, France, and Italy). There was little interaction between the units, and each was assigned a particular sector of the city.

Unilateral peace operations are often hard to distinguish from conventional military interventions. The major distinction lies in the range of functions performed by the soldiers; to the extent that it does not favor one side or the other in a conflict and carries out non-traditional missions such as humanitarian assistance, such a unilateral operation resembles a peace operation more than an invasion. A single state sends its military forces into an area, with the decision to intervene, the conduct of the operation, and ultimately the exit decision made by the national government. India's intervention into Sri Lanka is sometimes labeled as a peace operation. US actions in Somalia (UNITAF) and the French intervention in Côte d'Ivoire (Operation Licorne) respectively illustrate instances of largely unilateral operations that share some characteristics with peace operations. The International Force for East Timor (INTERFET) is one clear example of such a multinational peace operation.

INTERFET was authorized by the United Nations Security Council in September 1999, in the aftermath of East Timor's

Box 3.3 INTERFET

INTERFET was tasked with a peace enforcement Chapter VII mandate to use all necessary measures "to restore peace and security in East Timor."

Headquarters: Dili, East Timor

Duration: September 1999 – February 2000

Maximum Strength: 11,285

Cost: No reliable data available on the cost

pro-independence vote in an August 1999 referendum and the subsequent Indonesian-backed violence against the East Timorese. Acting under Chapter VII of the UN Charter, it was tasked with a peace enforcement mandate to use all necessary measures "to restore peace and security in East Timor, to protect and support UNAMET[5] in carrying out its tasks and, within force capabilities, to facilitate humanitarian assistance operations" (United Nations 1999). INTERFET was led by Australia, which provided about one-third of the approximately 11,000 peacekeepers, while another twenty states provided the rest of the multinational force. INTERFET deployed a robust presence in East Timor, with heavy armored vehicles, and engaged the anti-independence militias and the Indonesian security forces several times. This peace enforcement mission was meant to bridge the way for a United Nations peace operation to be deployed and help the East Timorese authorities with the independence process. INTERFET is hailed as a major peace operation success. There was a clear mandate from the UN Security Council to create peace and security within a limited time frame, and a clear leader of the multinational peace operation, Australia. This represents the typical multinational peace operation: clearly defined mandate, limited time frame, robust peace enforcement intervention, and a specific lead-country for the multinational force.

Configurations Involving Multiple Agents: Sequential, Parallel, and Hybrid Peace Operations

The institutional arrangements described above generally involve only one organizational setup, yet it has become more common for peace operations to be composed of several institutional agents. There are three types of arrangements that have been frequently used: sequential operations, parallel deployments, and hybrid peace operations. Another, less used, configuration of peace operations has several agents involved; certain actors or organizations provide the financing, logistics, airlift capability, and other elements of an operation, while other actors or organizations supply the troops on the ground and implement the mission. US President Clinton attempted to formalize this with his African Crisis Response Initiative, in which the USA would supply funding and training for peacekeepers from African states and organizations to carry out missions on their continent. More commonly, though, such arrangements are put in place on a case-by-case basis (e.g., NATO provided airlift capability and training for the African Union's peacekeepers in Darfur from 2005 to 2007).

Sequential operations occur when one peace mission performs certain duties in advance or immediately after the peacekeeping mission of a different agency. There are two types of sequential operations: bridging and hand-overs. "Bridging operations occur when one peace operation deploys rapidly for a short period of time and with a clear end-date, until another international organization steps in to take over the responsibilities" (Balas 2011a: 394). For example, an EU force, Operation Artemis (with France as the primary sponsor), was authorized by the UN Security Council to stabilize a given area of the DR Congo prior to the deployment of a UN mission (MONUC). This EU mission was deployed for only three months, with very specific goals, before the UN could find more peacekeepers to deploy in eastern DR Congo. Another example is the multinational military force in Haiti (primarily France and the USA) that paved the way for a UN operation (MINUSTAH). "Hand-over operations occur when one international organization withdraws its peace operation from a conflict to let another one take over those responsibilities" (ibid.). Hand-overs are not intended as quick fixes for a peace operation that does not have the capabilities to take care of a specific region of the conflict. Rather, they represent a change of responsibility for that conflict between different international agencies. For example, in Kosovo, an EU force, EULEX, took over from the United Nations, UNMIK, in 2009. Similarly, ECOMOG and ECOMICI operations from ECOWAS handed over the responsibility for peacekeeping in Liberia and Côte d'Ivoire to the UN.

Parallel deployments are represented by two or more peace operations from different agencies that position themselves in the same conflicts and have some temporal overlap. These operations are independent of each other and quite often are responsible for different aspects of peacekeeping (peace enforcement, peacebuilding) or for different sectors/ regions of the conflict zone. They each retain independent control over their decisions, resources, actions, and costs. For example, in Afghanistan, NATO has been conducting a peace enforcement operation, while the UN and the EU have deployed peacebuilding operations, during the same period, since 2003. In Georgia, from 1994 to 2008, OSCE focused on the conflict in South Ossetia, while the UN focused its peace operation on the adjacent conflict in Abkhazia.

A third institutional arrangement is a hybrid joint mission between international institutions, such as the arrangement in Sudan in which the UN and the AU deployed UNAMID, the African Union–United Nations Mission in Darfur. Hybrid peace operations are integrated missions that have a uni-

Box 3.4 UNAMID

UNAMID was a Chapter VII peace operation mandated to protect civilians, provide security for humanitarian assistance, contribute to the promotion of human rights and the rule of law, and monitor the implementation of the ceasefire/peace agreements.

Headquarters: El Fasher, Darfur, Sudan

Duration: From July 2007 (ongoing)

Maximum Strength: 20,888

Cost: approximately US$8.5 billion total (estimate)

fied, joint chain of command involving personnel from both institutions. All planning and decision-making go through the bureaucracies of both institutions. There are not many examples of such a hybrid operation, as it is a new model that seems to be cumbersome and not especially effective. The cases of hybrid peace operations are limited to three conflicts – Haiti (MICIVIH – the integrated OAS/UN operation), Sudan (UNAMID in Darfur), and Kosovo (the NATO/UN/OSCE integrated operations).

UNAMID, a typical example of a hybrid operation, took over the peacekeeping role from the African Union's mission in Sudan (AMIS) on December 31, 2007. The African Union was the first organization to send peacekeepers to the conflict that started in Darfur in 2003. These AU peacekeepers were initially military observers but, as the conflict escalated, the mandate was enlarged to include the protection of civilians. Nevertheless, the AU was not well equipped to deal with a conflict of these proportions.[6] AMIS was poorly financed and never managed to deploy the maximum number of peacekeepers proposed. Thus, the United Nations stepped in, first with help through UNMIS (deployed in Southern Sudan) and later through the creation of a hybrid peace operation. UNAMID took over all the personnel and equipment of AMIS. Its Chapter VII mandate was to protect civilians, provide security for humanitarian assistance, contribute to the promotion of human rights and the rule of law, and monitor the implementation of the ceasefire/peace agreements. Both the African Union and the United Nations had control over the operation. The UN Assistance Cell in the African Union Headquarters in Addis Ababa was established to embed a UN team within the structure of the African Union to improve coordination between the two organizations. The effectiveness of this hybrid peace operation is not clear. On the one hand, it has been successful in terms of providing legitimacy for the UN to get involved in the Darfur conflict at a time when the president of Sudan did not want to accept non-African peacekeepers. On the other hand, UN officials seem to think that this hybrid model is cumbersome and should not be repeated (Derblom, Frisell, and Schmidt, 2008). No new hybrid peace operations have been developed since UNAMID.

Inter-Organizational Cooperation in Peace Operations
Balas (2011a) defined peace operations in which two or more agents deploy their own separate peace operations at the same time, in the same conflicts, as multiple simultaneous peace operations (MSPOs). Balas (2011b) explores the rationale for cooperation between peace operations deployed in sequential, parallel, and hybrid settings. There are two stages for the initiation of inter-organizational cooperation in peace opera-

Table 3.2 Organizational forms of peace operations	
Type of peace operation	Number of operations
Single	78
Sequential (bridging)	11
Sequential (hand-overs)	12
Parallel	79
Hybrid	8

tions: the member state level and the organizational level respectively.

Member states of an international organization stand to gain from inter-organizational cooperation. They might increase control over their agents (international organizations), balance the risks of failure between different organizations, promote their preferred organization, and better serve national interests. Thus states rarely block inter-organizational cooperation, which has happened in only six out of ninety-nine cases (Balas 2011b): Turkey, a NATO member, and Cyprus, an EU member, blocked NATO–EU cooperation four times because of their dispute over northern Cyprus; and Russia blocked cooperation between the Commonwealth of Independent States and the EU's peace operations in Moldova and Georgia, respectively.

At the organizational level, cooperation occurs because of resources and complementarity of activities. The organizations that deploy just a few hundred peacekeepers on the ground join forces, quite often, with those that deploy several thousand troops in the same conflict. Cooperation also occurs when the organizations devote similar amounts of financial resources and implement similar peacekeeping activities. When the peacekeepers of different agencies find themselves in dangerous environments, they tend to collaborate with one another. However, we need to know more about the impact of complementarity and comparative advantage on inter-organizational cooperation. Balas (2011b) argues that there is no evidence for cooperation between peace operations with different mandates. On the contrary, cooperation occurs between two similar operations. For example, both the OSCE and the EU are conducting civilian peacebuilding in Bosnia. If one looks at the specific activities, there is complementarity and a comparative advantage. The OSCE is in charge of elections supervision and civil society training, while the EU is tasked with economic development and conflict transformation.

Other Alternatives
Other institutional arrangements for peace operations are conceivable. The most likely one is the employment of private contractors for certain functions. To some extent, this already occurs, as private agencies assist some peacebuilding operations. The provision of CIVPOL personnel, especially to train national constabulary forces, is a function most suited to private companies. Lawyer (2005) notes that the number of private military companies servicing peace operations has grown because of the security vacuum left by the end of the Cold War, the reduction in the size of national militaries, and the emergence of a norm of privatization for many international activities. Still, "private peacekeeping," as it is referred to, is generally more of a supplement than a replacement for other organizational forms of peace operations. Most likely, private firms will provide certain functions to peace operations, as DynCorp International has done in supplying civilian personnel to peace operations in Haiti and elsewhere.

It is also possible that some peace operations will be conducted remotely, without the use of peace soldiers and with the involvement only of technical personnel. Such tasks could be accomplished with existing agency frameworks or by private contractors. In all cases, however, the use of advanced technology is involved.[7] Monitoring technologies include a wide variety of different methods to detect and assess the movements of troops, civilians, and weaponry. Among above-ground technologies are aerial reconnaissance, commercial high-resolution satellite images, and remotely piloted vehicles, while among ground-based systems are various configurations using different kinds of radar (obviously linked in some cases with above-ground technologies), ground-based sensors (including sonar and seismic sensing), webcams, and different types of cameras. Other monitoring technologies are tags and active/passive seals for equipment and night-vision goggles for peacekeepers. All of the monitoring technologies are designed to detect improper troop movements, ceasefire violations, illegal weapons procurement, and the like. The general logic is that such methods are superior to what can be detected by on-site inspectors or through normal human vision at a distance.

A number of these technologies are already in use in peace operations. For example, the Multinational Force and Observers (MFO) operation in the Sinai employs night-vision devices to monitor movements in a demilitarized zone. Space-based monitoring was used in Bosnia. Nevertheless, the use of new technologies in peace operations is, at best, in its nascent stage. Too often, peacekeepers lack even the most rudimentary technologies, such as UNOSOM II commanders not having even simple telephones by which to communicate. Furthermore, there are few scenarios in which technology could fully replace existing peace operation agents. There are certain political and operational functions (e.g., many peace-building tasks) that technology could not perform, and most of those applying technology to peace operations view that technology as having a complementary rather than a substitution role.

Comparative Assessment

Which institutional arrangement is the best? As might be expected, there is no easy answer, and some agents may conduct better peace operations in some contexts as opposed to others. Furthermore, the next chapter provides an extended discussion of the conditions associated with peace operation success; most of those factors are unrelated to or unaffected by which organizational arrangement exists for the mission.

Indeed, regional organizations have no record of performance superior (or indeed inferior) to the UN in conflict management broadly.[8] Nevertheless, there is some evidence that peace operations differ in effectiveness according to the organizing agency, although one must note that UN peace operations are often sent to more difficult situations than are regional efforts (Wallensteen and Heldt 2008). In the discussion below, we focus primarily on the UN versus regional alternatives, although there are occasional references to multinational operations as well.

Compared to the heterogeneous members in the United Nations, states in a regional organization are assumed to be at the same developmental level, share historical, ethnic, or tribal roots, and have similar political outlooks flowing from facing common regional problems. These commonalities purportedly provide greater consensus among the members and make authorization of conflict management easier, as there will be fewer disagreements blocking strong action. Many also expect that regional organizations will receive more support from the disputants and the local population. Finally, regional peace operations may be better able to secure the support of the interested third-party states, which will almost assuredly participate in the debate and authorization of a regional operation, whereas they may not do so in a UN one. Such assumptions are perhaps why states and commentators call for regional solutions to problems ("African solutions for African problems"). Regional organizations are also not constrained, as is the UN, by the veto power of leading members. Indeed, some regional organizations have adopted procedures to avoid such a deadlock; the OSCE rule on "consensus minus one" allows it to take action against any one of its members. A multinational coalition might be either more or less desirable than a UN peace operation, depending on the breadth of the coalition and consent of the interested parties.

To the extent that regional operations can generate more support than UN missions, they have an important advantage, yet they must clear two hurdles that may frequently trip them up. First, the organization must reach sufficient consensus to authorize the mission in order to give it legitimacy, which is far from a foregone conclusion in most cases. Second, a regional organization must be accepted as an honest broker in the conflict. This again may be difficult to achieve. For example, any OAS operation that is led by the United States and that may serve US interests will have less legitimacy than a UN force. A Nigerian-led force in West Africa encounters similar difficulties, a situation evident in the ECOWAS operation in Liberia (ECOMOG). If the conflict at hand causes splits in the region as a whole, then any action is unlikely to receive authorization and, even if approved, may not be perceived as impartial by all parties. Thus, while the advantage of greater support is true in theory, it is less likely to be manifest in practice.

In practice, there have been great splits among members of regional organizations when dealing with regional conflicts. For example, the League of Arab States (LAS) was virtually paralyzed during the Iran–Iraq War and the Iraqi invasion of Kuwait, because its members were strongly divided in their loyalties to the protagonists. Regional animosities also tend to hamper regional organizations' actions. Unity from homogeneity comes in response to threats to security external to the organization, such as Arab unity against Israel or African support for decolonization in Angola. The most common threats that might prompt the deployment of a peace operation – internal threats – are exactly those least likely to generate consensus. Multinational operations do not necessarily depend on consensus for action, but peace operations are viewed as more legitimate when the coalition is larger as opposed to being seen as duties carried out primarily by a single state.

Relevant third-party states will almost assuredly participate in the debate and authorization of any regional peace
operation, whereas they may not in a UN forum. In this way,
third-party states have a better chance of modifying the operation according to their views and are more likely to support it.
More importantly, they are less likely to sabotage the organization's efforts. Although this advantage is by no means
guaranteed, the support of third-party states is a definite
benefit for regional operations and constitutes the primary
advantage of those operations over missions run by global
organizations or multinational configurations. Unless states
in the latter have taken actions to garner the support of other
parties, they too will suffer from potential opposition; the failure of the Multinational Force (MNF) to secure support from
various factions in Lebanon, and even supporting some factions over others, led to serious problems with the operation.

It may be the case that regional organizations or multinational coalitions are more willing to conduct peace operations
than the UN in some cases, but there are no systematic and
overwhelming advantages for those arrangements, at least
independent of context. There are, however, some significant
disadvantages in many cases, which suggest that, however
flawed UN operations might be, they have substantial relative
merits.

There is a strong risk that the difficulties the United
Nations has experienced in paying for operational activities
would be magnified in a regional operation. A regional operation would incur expenses similar to a UN operation but has
fewer states to draw upon for contributions. Each member has
to pay more than if the costs were borne on a global level; an
organization with a small membership could find the burden
crushing. As noted above, however, there is great variation in
regional organization capacity, and this potential disadvantage may be mitigated when comparing the most developed

regional organizations (e.g., the EU) against the UN. Resource constraints were most prominent in the OAU operations in Chad (e.g., Chad I). Many states failed to follow through on promises to support the peace force with troops and financial contributions. It is doubtful that subregional organizations could sustain an operation for an extended period without outside aid. Multinational coalitions will depend heavily on the resources provided by the states which supply the peace operation. If the coalition is large (e.g., the MFO) and/or the states are developed (e.g., Australia in East Timor), then few difficulties arise. A different configuration, however, subjects multinational operations to the same problems as the missions of small regional organizations.

A consistent theme in the analysis of regional organizations is their inability to take concerted action against their most powerful members. Regional operations are unlikely to be authorized in conflicts that directly involve the global or regional powers. The organization has neither the political clout nor the resources to mount an operation opposed or not actively supported by those states. A regional hegemon would be able to resist pressure to support a peace operation. Even if one were to be authorized, the hegemon could effectively sabotage the mission through direct action or covertly through intermediate actors. This condition necessarily confines strong regional responses to conflicts between or within smaller states. For example, the CIS will be unable to mount any effective operational action that is not supported by Russia. In general, only the UN offers the potential to restrain a regional power, although perhaps not a superpower. The UN has the resources, even without the cooperation of some states, and it has the political power to pressure states such as India to accede to its peace operations.

Although there has been a notable increase in the number of regional peace operations, this is not inherently good or bad. We know that regional organizations (e.g., KFOR in Kosovo) and multinational organizations (MFO in the Sinai) are capable of carrying out peace operations successfully just as much as they are prone to failure (e.g., ECOMIL in Liberia and MNF in Lebanon, respectively). The same might be said of UN operations. The benefits of one organizing agency over another are intimately tied to the kind of conflict, the local context, and a series of other factors affecting peace operations.

Personnel

With the possible exception of NATO, global and regional organizations do not have permanent forces at their disposal, and therefore troops and structures must be assembled on an ad hoc basis. Multinational coalitions draw upon personnel from national armies. Whatever the agency, however, it relies on its members to supply soldiers to any peace operation it authorizes. A list of selected ongoing operations as of 2012 and their troop levels is given in table 3.3. In this section, we explore what determines the personnel needs of peace operations and which states contribute soldiers to peace operations and why. We conclude with an assessment of alternative mechanisms for supplying peace operations, including those proposals under the rubrics of a permanent peace force or a rapid deployment force.

Perhaps because it has conducted so many operations, the UN has standard operating procedures for personnel supply and command, even as these are executed in an ad hoc and on a case-by-case basis. The institutional arrangements for UN peacekeeping operations are an amalgamation of national and international components. Soldiers are organized in national contingents under the direct command of military officers from their home countries. Decisions on redeployment or disciplinary action for code-of-conduct violations are also the

Table 3.3 Peace soldiers in selected ongoing operations, 2012

Acronym	Full mission name	Number of military personnel
UNMOGIP	UN Military Observer Group in India and Pakistan	40
UNAMA	UN Assistance Mission in Afghanistan	12
ISAF	International Security Assistance Force	131,730
UNMIK	UN Interim Administration Mission in Kosovo	8
KFOR	Kosovo Force	8,454
EUFOR	European Union Force – Althea	600
CPKF/CPFOR	CIS Collective Peacekeeping Force in Georgia/ Collective Peacemaking Force	2,542
OSCE Mission	OSCE Mission – Bosnia	0
	Moldova Joint Force/Joint Control Commission PK Force	1,402
	South Ossetia Joint Force	1,519
OSCE Mission	OSCE Mission – Georgia	0
MINUSTAH	UN Stabilization Mission in Haiti	7,032
UNTSO	UN Truce Supervision Organization	149
UNDOF	UN Disengagement Observer Force	1,045
UNIFIL	UN Interim Force in Lebanon	11,961
MINURSO	UN Mission for the Referendum in Western Sahara	236
MFO	Multinational Force and Observers	1,672
RAMSI	Regional Assistance Mission to the Solomon Islands	150
UNMIT	UN Integrated Mission in Timor-Leste	35
UNIPSIL	UN Integrated Peacebuilding Office in Sierra Leone	0
UNMIL	UN Mission in Liberia	8,069
UNOCI	UN Operation in Côte d'Ivoire	7,758
	Operation Lincorne	900

Source: SIPRI Multilateral Peace Operations Database, 2013.

responsibility of national military structures. Yet commanders of national contingents coordinate with and report to the overall UN force commander.

The UN system does, however, have a number of drawbacks. Efficiency suffers because coordination is difficult between national contingents with different languages, protocols, and levels of professionalism. UN forces also become subject to the political interests of the contributing states, which may restrict their forces from performing controversial actions, such as initiating attacks on local military groups. The supply of CIVPOL personnel poses particular problems, in that few states have reserve police personnel available for immediate duty, and many of those officers are not trained for duties and environments that are in many cases quite different from those in their homelands.

Historically, the AU and the EU have relied on similar, largely ad hoc arrangements for staffing peace operations. In the AU, the Chairperson of the Commission is assigned to assemble a force and seek voluntary contributions from member states. The EU traditionally signed agreements with third-party states to provide troops to peace operations, but, following the authorization of a particular mission, conferences are held to confirm precise contributions according to mission needs. The EU, however, is in transition with its Rapid Reaction Force, a quasi-permanent arrangement for 60,000 troops that had been many years in the planning but became operational only in 2007. Still, the force is not a standing army, but a series of commitments by EU members to have troops ready for deployment; nevertheless, member states can still decide to opt out of particular missions.

Predicting the Size of Peace Operations
What determines how many troops are deployed in a given peace operation? One would like to assume that the number

of soldiers and ancillary personnel is whatever is optimal for accomplishing the mission. In reality, however, the number of troops provided is a function of what the authorizing agency permits and the contributing states ultimately provide. Thus, there is a strong likelihood that actual troop numbers are suboptimal. Green, Kahl, and Diehl (1998a) analyzed UN operations and identified a series of factors associated with the size of peace operations. Although their study does not cover operations in the last decade or more, it does take in missions representing a wide range of tasks, including observation, traditional peacekeeping, and series of peacebuilding missions.

Most significantly, the type of mission performed by the peace operation has a major effect on troop strength. Traditional peacekeeping operations involved significantly more troops than observer missions. Most dramatically, peacebuilding missions tended to require almost double the troop levels of traditional missions. For example, NATO's KFOR mission in Kosovo had 45,000 uniformed personnel at its peak, with several thousand more in related missions in Macedonia and elsewhere. These figures do not even include civilian police, administrative personnel, and other support staff. In contrast, the traditional UNDOF mission on the Golan Heights between Israel and Syria has consistently hovered just above 1,000 military personnel.

Observation missions tend to be the smallest of the three operational types. Their more limited tasks generally require fewer personnel (for example, the OSCE mission in Moldova has never had more than ten observers). In contrast, traditional peacekeeping forces require more troops than observer missions, given that they have to perform an interposition function, and small numbers of personnel may not be enough to deter an attack or to monitor a ceasefire.

Peacebuilding operations involve more labour-intensive activities, such as humanitarian assistance or election supervision, than are required of a simple interposition force. Such operations may also need to be larger than other missions, given that they may be deployed in areas before fighting has stopped.

The conflict context, specifically its severity, is also associated with larger missions. The most severe conflicts inflate troop requirements, probably because more personnel are needed to facilitate and monitor ceasefires than in less hostile circumstances. Accordingly, the second phase of the MONUC operation in the Congo, starting in 2003, numbered more than 17,000 troops. The increase in actors in the conflict also has an additive effect on the number of troops in a UN peace operation: the greater the number of independent actors (both state and non-state), the greater the number of troops required. Multiple adversarial relationships will most likely require more troops to keep the peace in monitoring the activities of those additional belligerents. Green, Kahl, and Diehl (1998a) did not find that the type of conflict (for example, civil war vs. interstate war) necessarily affected the size of deployment, although, as noted in the next chapter, this distinction has implications for operation success.

In general, the geographical characteristics of the area where the troops are deployed do not affect force size. The exception is in the physical extent of the area of deployment, although the impact is not substantial. A geographically large area will necessitate a rather large force to monitor activities. The number of national borders and the physical terrain of the deployment area do not necessarily affect the number of soldiers allocated to a peace operation.

Who Provides Peacekeepers?
In a system that depends on ad hoc arrangements and the absence of troops under the control of the sponsoring agency, peace operations must depend on the voluntary contributions

of member states. Which states provide soldiers for such operations? Contributions are not equally distributed across all members of the international system or a region. This is not necessarily surprising. There is no mechanism (as there is for financing of operations – see below) to assess or compel contributions, so the system is vulnerable to "free riding" by some states. That is, some states will choose not to contribute troops to an operation, letting others shoulder the burden, while all enjoy the public goods of international peace and security. Nonetheless, there are some patterns in the provision of troops to peace operations.

In traditional operations and in the early years of the UN, peacekeeping troops were drawn primarily from states that did not have direct involvement in the conflict at hand. For example, the UNEF II operation relied on troop contributions from thirteen states (Australia, Austria, Canada, Finland, Ghana, Indonesia, Ireland, Nepal, Panama, Peru, Poland, Senegal, and Sweden), none of which was from the region or closely allied to participants in the Arab–Israeli conflict. That is, states that were closely aligned with any of the combatants or were close neighbors were excluded from participation. To do otherwise would jeopardize the perceived neutrality of the force. As soldiers were under national command, such soldiers might favor one side or the other in the conflict. As traditional missions depended on host-state consent to keep the peace, any bias, real or perceived, could unravel an operation, and fighting could be renewed. In keeping with the goal of preserving the neutrality of the force, Cold War operations also systematically excluded contributions from the superpowers and most of their allies; a number of conflicts to which peacekeepers were deployed, especially in the Middle East, were intimately tied to Cold War concerns. Still, peacekeeping missions often had troop contributions from one member of the Warsaw Pact (e.g., Poland) and one member of NATO (e.g., Canada), but generally no more. The role of providing peace soldiers fell heavily on so-called middle powers, such as Australia, Canada, and India. These states had the capability to provide well-trained personnel to peace missions but had no imperialist interests. Many of these states also saw participation in peace operations as part of their contributions to the international community, even as their influence in other aspects of international relations was less pronounced.

Multinational operations have been conditioned more by the context of the operation and the preferences of the disputing parties. For example, the MFO operation patrols the Sinai between Egypt and Israel. Because Israel regards the UN and most of its membership as biased against its interests, another UN operation was not possible in the aftermath of the Camp David Accords. Indeed, the mediator of those accords, the United States, is the largest troop contributor to the MFO force. Thus, it serves as a guarantor of the agreement between Egypt and Israel, and its participation in the MFO is part of that commitment – some may even say a prerequisite for the agreement itself.

In the post-Cold War era, some of the informal restrictions on participation have been lifted. Many European states are no longer involved in Cold War tensions and thus are more frequent contributors to peace operations. Still, for UN operations, the predominant contributions still come from those states which have been traditional suppliers. For operations in place in December 2012 (United Nations 2012), the top three contributing states to UN operations were Pakistan, Bangladesh, and India respectively; following some distance behind are Ethiopia, Nigeria, Rwanda, and Nepal.

More notable changes are evident in regional operations, in which contributions by regional powers or neighbors are more common. For example, Nigeria was a leading contributor to the ECOWAS-sponsored force in Liberia (ECOMOG).

Similarly, Russia has played a prominent role in peace missions authorized by the Commonwealth of Independent States (CIS): indeed, it was the sole provider of troops to the CIS Peacekeeping Force in Georgia, starting in 1994. Similarly, multinational missions may draw upon local powers and geographically proximate states. In the Regional Assistance Mission in the Solomon Islands (RAMSI), Australia and several neighbors were the states organizing and providing the forces. The willingness of states to provide troops and the capability for doing so in these situations have replaced primary concerns for neutrality in constituting peace forces.

The increased participation in peace operations by emerging powers such as Brazil, China, and South Africa[9] is not, as some analysts (Wiharta, Melvin, and Avezor 2012; Gill and Huang 2009) claim, the major change in peacekeeping. From 2003–4 to 2012, South Africa, Brazil and China did significantly expand their participation in peace operations, ranking constantly in the top twenty UN peace operations troops-contributing countries. China, for example, increased its personnel contributions from 123 civilian police and military observers in 2002 to 1,036 military peacekeepers in 2004. Nevertheless, countries with small militaries, such as Rwanda, Uruguay, Jordan, and Nepal, have consistently contributed approximately twice as many peacekeepers as Brazil or China every year since 2004. Also, Brazil's contributions to peacekeeping are tied to one single mission: MINUSTAH in Haiti. South Africa's contributions involve two major peace operations in Africa – DR Congo and Darfur, Sudan. Three-quarters of China's peacekeepers were deployed in peace operations in Africa, especially in Liberia, South Sudan/ Sudan, and DR Congo. Thus, the increase in troop contributions from Brazil, China, and South Africa, as welcome as it may be, remains small, and the impact on peace operations as a whole is still quite limited.

The motivations for state participation in peace operations are multifaceted. Neack (1995) argues that "realist" rather than "idealist" motives are dominant in states' decisions to contribute troops. As peace missions, especially regional operations, serve the interests of certain states, these states will be more likely to contribute troops. Wiharta, Melvin, and Avezor (2012) contend that Brazil and South Africa are two examples of states that assert their regional power through their involvement in peace operations in the Americas and Africa, respectively. A number of peace operations serve the continuation of the international status quo and foster certain liberal values such as democratization. Accordingly, some more advanced Western and non-Western states have seen contributing to peace operations as a way to promote their own interests and values; NATO's KFOR operation in Kosovo and the ISAF operation in Afghanistan, both initiated primarily by Western allies, are prime examples. Non-Western states such as China have contributed peacekeepers to African conflicts in order to boost their international standing (Gill and Huang 2009) and to continue extracting African raw materials needed by its growing economy. For other states, the self-interested motivations are different. Smaller states, such as Fiji, gain significant international prestige from participation in peace operations. Their soldiers also receive training and field experience they might otherwise not obtain in any other way. Finally, contributing troops to a peace operation can actually be profitable for some states. Countries receive a flat-rate payment from the UN for each soldier in a peace mission, and many pay their soldiers at a lower national rate, pocketing the difference.

Proposals for a Peace Force

Were one to design an optimal system for the provision of troops to a peace operation, it would not resemble status quo arrangements. Military establishments around the world no longer rely on citizen soldiers who voluntarily leave the fields to fight when conflicts arise. Professional armies replaced such ad hoc arrangements in the international system over the seventeenth and eighteenth centuries. Why hasn't the international community devised a better arrangement for its peace operations?

The idea of greater force readiness for peace operations is hardly new and has taken many forms over the years. In the sections below, we outline some of those proposals and the reasons why they have yet to be adopted. We conclude with an assessment of the likely impact that such plans would have on the effectiveness of future peace operations.[10]

A History of Peace Force Proposals

The idea of a permanent peace force has extended roots in the post-World War II era. According to Article 43 of the UN Charter, members were to make available to the Security Council troops and materiel to be used in the organization's enforcement actions. The inability of the superpowers to agree on the details of the plans meant that the provisions of Article 43 never reached fruition. Although such forces were intended as military units rather than as peacekeeping troops, the concept of an international force was envisioned by the framers of the Charter.

Recognizing the need for an international force, but also understanding that the superpowers could not agree on one that involved collective security, Trygve Lie, the UN Secretary-General, offered a path-breaking proposal in the late 1940s. He suggested that an international force be created, based upon the model of observer groups then operating in the Middle East. This was the beginning of the movement for a permanent international force that was not designed for collective security purposes. Even such a limited plan, however, failed to gain the approval of the Security Council, and of the Soviet Union in particular. Shortly thereafter, the General Assembly did approve a "shadow force" consisting of names of potential recruits for international observer missions; the collection of such names, however, never took place. It is notable in this instance that plans for a permanent force quickly gave way to a less far-reaching proposal. This scenario was to be repeated several times over the next decades.

Many ideas, including those of Secretary-General Dag Hammarskjöld, focused on standby forces, akin to military reserves, that could be activated on short notice. Although many sources expressed support for the general concept, disagreements between the superpowers again negated any possibility for the creation of such a force.

In the early 1960s, Canadian Under-Secretary of State for Foreign Affairs Lester Pearson, who was instrumental in the formation of UNEF I, proposed creating standby forces, perhaps through the joint efforts of several states. Again, this represented a concession to the reality that more ambitious proposals would fail. This suggestion called only for a standby force, not a standing force. Furthermore, the proposal suggested that the UN might not have a primary role in the formation of peacekeeping units, a job to be left to a consortium of interested states under a multilateral agreement.

Over the last several decades, various proposals for improving force readiness have been quite limited, but, even so, they have not been adopted. Many plans have advocated that states earmark troops for peace operations, with those troops available on short notice should they be required; this is one step below the level of readiness achieved with standby forces. This arrangement would still necessitate a UN mission organized on an ad hoc basis, but the troops would presumably have had some training in peacekeeping techniques and would also be more readily available. Still, the individual states control most of the training and supply aspects of the force.

In 1992, UN Secretary-General Boutros Boutros-Ghali revived the idea of an international standing force that could assume traditional peacekeeping and other duties. On the one hand, his proposal was limited, in that it essentially provided for the equivalent of standby troops, ready for deployment in a crisis. Yet Boutros-Ghali also envisioned these forces as "peace enforcement units" which could take on more coercive missions against states which threaten international security or violate ceasefires. Furthermore, he called for the reactivation of Article 43 and its Military Staff Committee to direct such operations. Although quite ambitious, the plan never generated significant support from key Security Council members. In the aftermath of the Rwanda genocide, the Netherlands proposed a "rapid deployment brigade" that would be a permanent force ready for action in preventive deployments, prior to the arrival of regular peace forces, and in humanitarian emergencies; speed in response to impending disasters was its main attribute. As with all other proposals, opposition from key states, such as the USA, prevented its adoption.

In general, the most ambitious proposals include provisions for a peace force that would be truly international in character. The force would be composed of international officials (military personnel and civil servants) who would be trained jointly, stationed together, and immediately available for duty; such an international army might roughly parallel national efforts at defense, except that units would have less of an enforcement role or none at all. Less extensive proposals advocate standby peacekeeping troops. In practice, this would involve forces that might or might not have joint training but would include pre-designated national troops for rapid deployment to any area of the world. A less formal commitment is the idea of earmarking troops for peacekeeping assignments. Here, a state would plan ahead so that a set number of its military personnel would be available for duty.

Some proposals dictate that UN soldiers undergo a rigorous training regimen under international auspices. Specialized training for peace operations is necessary because the attitudes, methods, and tactics differ significantly from conventional military doctrine. Proposals range from a training center for national units run by the UN to a regular training schedule pursued by a standing international force. Joint multinational training, such as that presently undertaken by the Nordic countries, is another possibility. The most limited form would involve national training for operation assignments as part of every soldier's preparation, or at least for those who might be assigned such duties.

A permanent peace force requires a well-developed infrastructure for logistical support. Various proposals advocate warehouses that can store necessary equipment and materiel. A more limited idea would be for UN staff to secure prior commitments from states to supply certain items or assistance; for example, an industrialized state might be well suited to provide assistance in setting up a communications network. Some proposals are so detailed that they even discuss how to provide soldiers with their native foods. All the plans that address logistics emphasize enhanced preparedness. Most of the alleged benefits from a permanent peace force stem from the advantages attendant on increased preparedness. In this way, most advocates emphasize the operational rather than the political benefits of such a force. Such advantages include enhanced professionalism, reaction time, efficiency, and financial stability. Of course, as one moves down the continuum to more limited proposals vis-à-vis the current status, the corresponding advantages are also reduced.

An Evaluation of Proposals
There are certainly some attractive features to a permanent peace force. Indeed, the assumption is that such a force is, *a priori*, a good idea, a line of thought reflected by James Boyd: "It is difficult to argue against the intrinsic value of having a permanently constituted force" (1971: 223). Yet, while a permanent force is preferable to the present ad hoc arrangement, it is not clear that the benefits are dramatic.

Although current forces do not receive the kind of training proposed under the most ambitious plans, they are not necessarily inexperienced in peace operation matters. Many troops receive suitable training in their own countries. Some states or groups of states already have extensive training programs. Furthermore, there have already been enough peace operations to create a large body of soldiers with prior experience now available for future duty. Training and experience among soldiers vary widely at the time of deployment. Problems with criminal acts committed by peacekeepers, including rape and looting, have occurred. Although they have been highly publicized, such incidents are not widespread, and it is unclear whether expanded training would have prevented them or not.

Another feature of a permanent peace force is rapid deployment following mission authorization. If one assumes the maximum efficiency of such a force, then this point holds. Yet, once again, the performance of troops under the present ad hoc arrangement is not as far from that standard as one might imagine. Experience has shown that, barring disagreements over financing or other matters, some troops are on the ground and in place between the combatants only a few days after authorization. Indeed, Canadian troops arrived in Cyprus within 24 hours of UNFICYP's approval. When there has been delay in the deployment of forces, as in the Congo or in Sudan, it has been the reluctance of contributing states (for fear of soldier safety) or the opposition of the host state that has delayed deployment rather than the unavailability of a rapid deployment force. Some arguments behind a rapid deployment brigade are that such a force could prevent genocide. Although this is a noble idea, it ignores that UN and NATO forces were already on the ground in Rwanda and Bosnia respectively when atrocities occurred. Although there may be multiple explanations for these tragedies, they do not include peace forces being unavailable. In addition, the availability of a standing force is irrelevant if the agency, be it the UN or a regional organization, is unwilling to authorize its use.

A permanent peace force backed up by better advanced planning and a full-time staff would undoubtedly be more efficient that the present system. Nevertheless, there needs to be more than a comparative advantage to justify a permanent force as regards this point. A more stringent criterion is that the advantage gained must be critical to the success of the mission. In the case of improved efficiency, problems with command, control, and coordination in previous operations have been relatively minor, often concerning problems over communication with troops with different native tongues and establishing lines of command across national contingents; such problems have never caused a peace operation to fail.

The final pillar on which the argument for a permanent peace force rests is financial stability. Such reasoning is flawed because it assumes that financial problems are separable from all other operational problems. In actuality, the willingness or reluctance of states to contribute to the support of a particular peace mission is a reflection of their political support for the operation. Historically, states withholding or withdrawing their financial support or troops signaled an erosion of political support for the mission among key elements of the UN membership. An alternative and autonomous method of funding, beyond member contributions, does not address the underlying problem of dissatisfaction or opposition from some significant states. The resulting hardships from financial instability have not been severe; even the accumulation of a large UN debt from past operations has not necessarily seriously hindered the conduct of existing operations or the authorization of new ones.

A permanent peace force has some advantages, but its marginal utility is not substantial. As is evident from the historical record, the present ad hoc system has performed reasonably well, given the difficult circumstances. Indeed, it offers the advantage of flexibility and adaptability in organizing operations. Many of the problems it has encountered have been minor or the result of factors that would not be resolved by the imposition of a permanent force. A permanent force would be more efficient and professional, and its reaction time would be improved. Surely, given the choice, most would favor such a force over current arrangements. Of course, much of this analysis is highly speculative and likely to remain that way. With the exception of the EU, there is no immediate prospect of any organization establishing a permanent peace force. States have generally been unwilling to create such an entity, preferring to retain political control over peace operations on a case-by-case basis.

Financing

Another element of the organization of peace operations is their financing. The cost of these operations is relatively low in comparison with national military budgets. For example, the fiscal year 2010 budget for UNTSO was only US$30 million, whereas the annual cost of the US occupation in Iraq was

Table 3.4 Financial cost of selected ongoing operations, 2012		
Acronym	Full mission name	Projected annual cost in US$ million
UNMOGIP	UN Military Observer Group in India and Pakistan	8.07
UNAMA	UN Assistance Mission in Afghanistan	238.60
ISAF	International Security Assistance Force	459.63
KFOR	Kosovo Force	38.01
OSCE Mission	OSCE Mission – Bosnia	14.97
MINUSTAH	UN Stabilization Mission in Haiti	611.75
UNTSO	UN Truce Supervision Organization	30.35
UNDOF	UN Disengagement Observer Force	45.03
UNIFIL	UN Interim Force in Lebanon	518.71
MINURSO	UN Mission for the Referendum in Western Sahara	60.04
MFO	Multinational Force and Observers	78
RAMSI	Regional Assistance Mission to the Solomon Islands	152.06
UNMIT	UN Integrated Mission in Timor-Leste	206.31
UNMIL	UN Mission in Liberia	525.05
UNOCI	UN Operation in Côte d'Ivoire	484.08
	Operation Licorne	95.62

Source: SIPRI Multilateral Peace Operations Database, 2013.

approximately $100 billion in yearly defense operational costs alone. Yet peace operation costs have escalated dramatically over the past two decades, even surpassing expenditures in the regular UN budget in the 1990s. The yearly costs of selected peace operations ongoing as of 2012 are given in table 3.4.

The Current System of Financing Peace Operations
Unlike many governments or organizations, the UN and other agents do not have one standard system for funding

their peace operations. In part, this is because peace operations tend to be organized on an ad hoc basis according to events breaking onto the world scene. Thus, the system of troop provision is mirrored in the financial arrangements that support such missions.

Although peace missions are organized on a case-by-case basis, this should not imply that the method of financing is random or completely unique to the operation at hand. Despite some variation across missions, UN operations are financed through several different mechanisms. One way is to meet expenses out of the regular UN budget. This is characteristic of the funding pattern for several observation missions, including the United Nations Truce Supervision Organization (UNTSO). Nevertheless, this mechanism is problematic when a particular mission is very expensive (and observation missions are usually smaller and cheaper than traditional or peacebuilding operations) or when the organization must handle several operations at once. Having peace operations compete with other UN priorities complicates the ability of the organization to fulfill its multifaceted mission, and is a poor solution all around in the face of severe budgetary pressures for the organization as a whole. Some indirect costs still remain under the rubric of the general budget, as political officers and the other members of the Secretariat assist missions in a variety of ways. Some early missions also had their costs borne by the disputants. This is a risky proposition, in that the protagonists may be too poor to afford a peace mission or to use their financial muscle to manipulate the conduct of the operation.

With the development of operations more expansive than simple observer missions, the UN funded traditional peacekeeping out of mission-specific special accounts; member states paid an assessment based on a formula similar to the one used for the regular budget, although this has varied over time, with all the money going to the peace operation. For the period 2013 to 2015, the top five contributors to UN peace operations were the United States (27.14 percent), Japan (12.53 percent), the United Kingdom (8.15), Germany (8.02 percent), and France (7.55 percent); except for Germany and France, all were significantly in arrears for their contributions at the end of 2010 (United Nations 2010). Accordingly, this has not always proven reliable, as states that object to a given operation may decide to withhold funds. The case of the United Nations Interim Force in Lebanon (UNIFIL) is illustrative. UNIFIL was originally funded out of a special account, but some states refused to pay their assessment for political reasons, and the operation quickly acquired a significant operating deficit. Less than two years after the UNIFIL deployment, the UN General Assembly created a "Suspense Account for UNIFIL" to supplement the special account. It was to be financed by voluntary contributions from member states, international organizations, and private sources and was to be used solely for reimbursing states that contributed troops to UNIFIL. Other missions receive voluntary contributions, including cash funds or contributions in kind (such as helicopters and other equipment). The obvious problem with voluntary funds, however, is that they can be quickly withdrawn at the whim of the contributors. Thus, both special accounts and mechanisms to supplement special accounts have their flaws, and neither has proved adequate for peace operations.

The EU and the AU operate under very different models from each other for financing their peace operations. The EU has a funding mechanism for what are classified as common costs – those expenses borne by the organization as a whole and not specific to any particular troop contributions. Such expenses are assessed to the EU membership, with the largest states (based on gross national product) bearing the greatest burden; for 2006, these were Germany (21.11 percent), France

(16.44 percent), Italy (13.64 percent), and the United Kingdom (13.05 percent). This funding mechanism is activated with the approval of missions. Non-common costs are paid according to the "costs lie where they fall principle"; effectively, this means that states pay for the troops that they agreed to contribute to the mission. Unlike the UN arrangements, in which some states have financial incentives to contribute soldiers, the EU provides something of a disincentive to offer troops to any peace missions.

The AU is composed of a significantly poorer set of states, and its financing mechanism reflects this. The AU's Peace Fund draws contributions from a host of sources, among them voluntary contributions from member states and other contributions from the continent, including from the private sector, civil society organizations, and individuals. Yet, given the poverty of the member states and the incentives to free ride, the organization cannot sustain its peace operations from these sources alone. Accordingly, the Chairman of the Commission also solicits contributions from outside Africa, most notably from other international organizations such as the UN and the EU. Indeed, for the AMIS operation, such voluntary contributions made up the largest portion of the budget. The AU pledges to reimburse costs to contributing member states, but, in the case of a shortfall, the organization may assess members or ask contributing states to bear costs unless funds become available. Thus, relying on member financing is the fallback position.

Many financial problems for peace operations are short term. The payment schedule for members' assessments does not necessarily conform to the timing of national budget allocations or the changing needs of the sponsoring agency, and as a result there are temporary shortfalls. Also, increased demands for new peace operations create short-term funding problems, as the authorizing agency must scramble to gain authorization and assemble a peace force on short notice. More serious are the long-term funding problems for operations. Some of these are caused by the rise in the number of ongoing peace operations. Some member states are too poor or experience sudden financial difficulties that make them unable to meet assessment schedules or to contribute voluntarily to peace operations. Most important is the unwillingness of states specifically to fund peace operations adequately. This leads to missing payment deadlines, a reluctance to authorize the necessary mandate if such authorization would result in higher expense, and an unwillingness to make voluntary payments to help support peace missions. The pecuniary and political sources of the financial problems are a direct consequence (although not a necessary one) of reliance on members' contributions for the funding of peace operations.

Predicting the Cost of Peace Operations
What determines the financial cost of peace operations to the sponsoring agency? This is a critical element for the organization conducting the operation and its members. Being able to estimate the costs of an operation will affect whether the organization is willing to take on a significant financial commitment. It is also essential to make an accurate cost–benefit analysis, which presumably is one factor that decision-makers consider when authorizing a peace mission. Yet most expectations of mission costs are inadequate at the time of deployment because of the great uncertainty associated with the likely length of the mission and possible changes in the tasks that might be performed.

Green, Kahl, and Diehl (1998b) identified several sets of factors that influenced the cost of UN operations. The length of a mission and the number of troops deployed are the key influences on peace force expenditures. Other things being equal, those missions that linger tend to cost more. The

UNTSO and UNFICYP missions have been in place for more than sixty and forty years respectively. Although the annual costs of those operations may be relatively low, the total accumulated costs are relatively great. There is no evidence that decision-makers have accurate predictions at the time of authorization of mission duration, and therefore the ultimate costs may come as a surprise to those who foot the bill. Still, if the cost is paid over a long period of time, the burden may be lessened, and in fact decision-makers may evaluate a mission more by its yearly costs than by its total costs.

As the main expenditures of peace operations are on personnel, it is not surprising that those missions with larger forces cost more than those with fewer soldiers. Of course, the size of a peace force is within the control of the authorizing agency and therefore can be manipulated to limit costs.

Traditional peacekeeping missions are more expensive than observer missions, and peacebuilding missions are the most expensive of all types (even controlling for force size). Observation missions tend to be the least costly because of their more limited tasks. In contrast, traditional peacekeeping forces require more troops than observer missions, given that they have to perform an interposition function, and small numbers of personnel may not be enough to deter an attack or to monitor a ceasefire. Peacebuilding missions, such as election supervision or humanitarian assistance, are more labor intensive than are those involving a simple interposition force. This necessarily leads to greater expense, and many of these missions have a significant civilian component and attendant staff costs that drive up the bill paid by organization members. Peacebuilding operations may also need to be larger than other missions, given that they may be deployed in areas before fighting has stopped; such situations may be more chaotic and less subject to host-state control. Of course, peacebuilding missions include significant costs, too, in the form of economic and development aid – expenses that are above and beyond those directly related to the operational components of the mission.

Conflict and actor characteristics do not affect the fiscal costs of operations, except indirectly as they relate to duration and troop strength. More severe conflicts require more time to solve (because of greater hostility and a tendency for disputant positions to harden) and may necessitate a larger number of troops to supervise ceasefires or carry out other tasks. Civil conflicts may involve more intractable discord over indivisible issues than purely interstate conflicts, leading to protracted fighting and larger peace force deployments. The greater the number of independent actors, the higher are the costs of operations. As with third-party states, the more actors actually or potentially involved in a dispute, the greater the expenses in monitoring the activities of those additional belligerents. Geographic factors do not seem to influence total peace force costs, although one would intuitively expect a larger deployment area to generate increased costs.

For policymakers seeking to reduce the costs of peace operations, one way is to attempt to manipulate them directly by setting real deadlines for troop withdrawal and authorizing the minimum number of troops thought necessary; this is especially relevant for those organization members most politically sensitive to the fiscal costs of peace operations – namely, the Western democracies and those organizations with limited resources, such as the AU. Yet there is the risk that, in deploying too few soldiers, the goals of the mission cannot be achieved. It was clear that 500 Pakistani peacekeepers in UNOSOM I were inadequate to deal with the situation in Somalia. Setting specific deadlines for withdrawal may also encourage parties to a conflict to use that deadline to stall or manipulate negotiations in contravention of the goal of peaceful conflict resolution. Early withdrawal of forces may be counterproductive to the long-term stability of a region. Furthermore, the use of civilian police and support staff as a replacement for soldiers, increasingly common in newer UN operations, leads to higher costs rather than net savings.

Proposals for Funding Peace Operations
As with the supply of peace soldiers, the funding mechanism for peace operations is not one of optimal design. Accordingly, there have been a number of proposals to change peace operation funding and indeed funding for international organizations in general. Yet an assessment of proposals to improve the financing of operations must take into account the context in which such reforms would occur. The general contexts in which the UN and regional organizations operate are those in which the organizations are subordinate to the interests of their members, most notably the powerful states. The limited autonomy of organizations may be a significant constraint on their abilities to enact the proposals outlined below.

First, legally, any major change in UN financing may require revisions to the UN Charter. Amendments to the UN Charter require two-thirds approval by member states, including all the permanent members of the Security Council (the United Kingdom, France, Russia, China, and the United States). Effectively, the five permanent members have a veto over Charter reform. Given the domestic political opposition in the United States and its Congress, it might be presumed that few proposals would gain American approval. Those that would result in greater US contributions to the organization appear to have the greatest hurdles to acceptance. Depending on the USA to provide leadership in the UN and spearhead financing reforms is unrealistic; that the USA would acquiesce in major changes to the organization is no more credible. Regional organizations may face similar, albeit less dire, legal and political limits on changing funding formulas.

Second, and beyond considerations of major power interests, financing reforms must find a balance between preserving and eroding state sovereignty. Member states are likely to oppose measures that give too much autonomy to the global or regional organizations. For example, on the one hand, there is suspicion that the UN cannot manage its own financial affairs properly, and member states want to be able to exercise control over disbursements. On the other hand, doubts about UN management aside, most member states will resist greater UN autonomy for political reasons. States find it in their interests to withhold contributions in order to exercise influence within the organization. Financial reforms that grant more autonomy to the organization eliminate or diminish that power, and one might expect that major contributors, especially the USA vis-à-vis the UN, will block efforts that tip the balance too far in the direction of greater organizational autonomy. Similar concerns are evident within regional organizations, except perhaps with respect to the EU. That association has already been delegated significant political and financial authority by its member states, and greater autonomy in the area of peace operations would seem to encounter fewer hurdles than in other regions.

Third, organizing agencies for peace operations are inherently constrained by a classic "free rider" problem. Many states will not contribute their share and will withhold funds for a collective good (here international peace and security) with the expectation that those states with the greatest stakes in the situation will provide the necessary funding anyway. The lack of an effective enforcement to pressure or punish recalcitrant states exacerbates the tendency. Thus, to the extent that financial reforms are accepted by the membership, we must recognize that there may be some slippage in implementation that leads to suboptimal effects.

Various authors and commissions have made or described proposals for improving financing, usually in the UN context and often generally and not necessarily specifically to peace operations.[11] Nonetheless, most of these ideas are applicable to peace operations, and similar plans could be adopted by regional organizations as well.

Incremental Change Proposals
One set of proposals shares the common feature of making only incremental changes to the existing ways of financing operations. None of these ideas represents dramatic overhauls of the size or source of funds, but rather they are best viewed as attempts to fine-tune problematic elements of the current system.

Late payment charges   One suggestion for ensuring timely payment of assessments (much of UN debt is attributable to states failing to pay assessments) is the imposition of fees or penalties for late payments. The hope is that such penalties will persuade balky contributors to pay their dues on time because there is a significant cost–benefit incentive not to delay (under the current system, there may even be some economic incentives not to pay on time). The rationale is quite similar to those employed by financial institutions which apply penalties or interest to late payments on credit cards, loans, and the like.

Changing payment dates   Another suggestion focuses on the payment schedule of member states. For example, the UN establishes assessments at the beginning of its fiscal year and requires members to pay their dues for the regular budget by January 31 of each year. A similar schedule is in effect for UN peace operations, although they do not necessarily arise or terminate on a regular schedule each year. Some states do not pay their assessments until after their own fiscal years have begun, often significantly later than the end of January deadline for the United Nations. The United States, for example, never makes any of its payments until the beginning of the American fiscal year in October, and Japan, another large contributor, waits until about June of each year to pay its assessments. One proposal would be to change the single due date for assessments to four quarterly instalment dates.

Modifying Article 19   Article 19 of the UN Charter stipulates that any UN member in arrears in the amount of two years' dues will lose its vote in the General Assembly. A suggested revision to that provision is to lower the debt amount that triggers the loss of voting privileges from two years to one year. The logic of this proposal is similar to that of the late payment penalty. It is hoped that the imposition of a sanction will induce member states to meet their obligations.

Changing the assessment schedule   A further suggestion deals with altering the method used to calculate the assessments that stipulate how much each state will pay to the UN budget or a given UN peace operation. The simplest idea is to use a three-year rather than a ten-year average of GDP in setting the assessments, with the logic that the shorter period is a more recent and therefore more accurate indicator of ability to pay. An alternative involves rearranging the assessment so that the largest burden does not fall on the most powerful states. The United States in particular, as well as its allies, pays a large share of the UN regular budget and an even larger share of peace expenses. Providing a flatter distribution of assessments across countries would make peace operations less of a hostage to withholding by any one state. Together with the three-year GDP modification, such a system might also be perceived as fairer, and thus large contributors might be more politically willing to honor financial commitments that they regard as legitimate.

Increasing the Working Capital Fund   The Working Capital Fund (WCF) was established in the UN's original financial plan to cover regular budget and limited emergency expenditures. This fund was originally larger than the regular budget but now is considerably less (over the years, the regular budget has expanded to reflect broader UN mandates and has been adjusted for inflation, whereas the WCF has increased only slightly). The UN taps funds from the WCF when member states are late paying their dues, and the fund is replenished when states finally pay their dues in full. One proposal is to increase the WCF, with each member state being assessed a one-time charge. This "rainy day" fund would hopefully allow the organization to meet emergencies better and ease problems that accompany short-term budget shortfalls, especially for peace operations.

Allowing the UN to borrow funds   A common method for businesses and governments to raise funds, especially on a short-term basis, is to borrow money. With respect to the UN, one proposal is to allow the organization to borrow funds from commercial institutions or other international lending agencies. A variation would accord Special Drawing Right (SDR) privileges to the UN similar to those enjoyed by state members of the International Monetary Fund. The borrowed funds would be used to make up for depleted funds until UN members paid their dues. Such an arrangement is not unprecedented for an international organization. The World Bank raises part of its capital by loans on the international capital markets.

Allowing the UN to sell bonds   Another favorite mechanism of governments and corporations to raise funds has been the sale of bonds. Under another proposal, the UN would be given this authority. Nevertheless, issuing bonds is merely another way of borrowing money, as the principal and interest must be repaid, although bonds do open up a broader creditor market than traditional loans. Yet one would expect that the same drawbacks as noted above for loans would be applicable to the sale of UN bonds. Indeed, in 1961, the General Assembly gave the Secretary-General authority to sell up to $200 million in bonds in order to meet shortfalls in two peacekeeping operations. Yet these entailed long-term debt (over twenty-five years), and some members withheld some payments to the UN that they believed were going for the repayment of the bonds.

The revolving peace fund   UN peace operations require funds before the UN can begin each mission, and often there is not substantial advance notice for such operations. Indeed, it may take several weeks for the UN to obtain the necessary emergency funds, leading to significant delay or complications for the operation, as was the case in the early stages of the UN operation in Bosnia. The UN has created a revolving peace fund for emergency peace operations. Common to many analysts' suggestions for UN reform is increasing the amount of the revolving peace fund.

An assessment of incremental change   Most of the incremental changes suggested for improving the financing of peace operations (or the organization as a whole) address only one small aspect of a larger problem. In that sense, even if they were to work as planned, the impact of any one change would be slight. Collectively, they offer the prospect of a more efficient organization, one that is less subject to the worst short-term shocks of under-funding. Yet, singularly or collectively, they all fail to provide the funds needed for current and expanded peace operations, and none is able to overcome the political and economic barriers that cripple the abilities of the UN and regional organizations to raise funds. Because they essentially rely on fine-tuning status quo mechanisms, they remain constrained by the weakest parts of the current funding system.

International Taxes

A second category of proposals frees organizations and their peace operations from dependence on members' contributions, the primary source of the financial problems. Instead, organizations would raise revenue in a fashion common to most national or local governance structures: the imposition of taxes or duties on various international entities or activities. Most tax plans would not make financing completely autonomous of their members, as those states would presumably determine the rates and applications of any international taxes as well as be responsible for the collection of those duties. Nevertheless, these various proposals represent a fundamental break with traditional methods of financing international organization activities of any variety (except perhaps for that related to seabed mining), and in particular peace operations. There are several variations on the idea of international taxes, which differ primarily with regard to the goods or services on which they might be levied.

Tobin tax   Among the most prominent international tax suggestions has been that proposed by the Nobel laureate economist James Tobin. Although his proposal was broadly designed to fund a range of UN activities, it could easily be modified to apply only to peace and security operations. Tobin's idea was to institute a small uniform tax on foreign exchange transactions. A low tax rate would have a negligible economic impact on international financial flows but still be able to raise large amounts of revenue, given the tremendous size of international exchange transactions that occur regularly on the international market.

International commons tax   An alternative form of taxation is the imposition of taxes or user fees in relation to the global commons. Global commons are defined as areas or resources that are the collective property of mankind and not under the sovereignty of any one state (e.g., most of the oceans or outer space). Among the various international commons tax proposals are those that include (a) sea routes, (b) exploration and work in the Antarctic, (c) airspace, (d) outer space, including satellites, (e) environmental pollution, (f) international transfer of genetic resources, and (g) fishing rights. The imposition of global commons taxes or user fees is not without precedent. The Seabed Authority under the Law of the Sea Treaty is funded by fees that are effectively taxes on mining and other activities in the global ocean commons.

Transnational activities tax   A variation of taxing usage of the global commons is imposing duties on transnational activities that usually do not involve common international property. Some examples of such activities are (a) international air travel (e.g., airport departure taxes), (b) air freight packages, (c) international telecommunications, (d) international postal services, (e) conventional arms sales, and (f) any of a number of categories of international trade.

An overview of international taxes   International taxes have the strength of being able to raise a large amount of revenue rather easily. With respect to international peace operations, the costs of the operations are not large compared to the budgets of major corporations or national governments or the value of various international transactions. Thus, one might predict that the tax rates would be very low and likely have little or no economic impact on the transactions themselves. Because corporations and other wealthy actors, rather than poor countries, are the ones which assume the financial burden, the system is thus less subject to the financial exigencies of its members. Furthermore, the tax rates could be modified to meet ebbs and flows in the demands for peace operations, making them more flexible than any of the incremental changes noted above.

The viability of any international tax scheme will depend heavily on the cooperation of the member states. Most obviously, the latter will be the entities responsible for collecting the revenues, and the risk of withholding those funds will still exist, although perhaps not as strongly as with direct contributions. More significant is whether governments will allow international agencies to have a quasi-independent financial capacity. The proposal of Secretary-General Boutros-Ghali for an international tax received harsh criticism from political leaders in the United States. Many states view this limited taxing capacity as the first step on a "slippery slope" toward greater autonomy for the organization.

New Programs and Ideas
A third category of proposals represents a dramatic break with past funding initiatives. These proposals are specifically geared toward the area of peace and security, whereas several of the previous ideas addressed generic problems of funding in the UN and regional organizations.

Self-financing   One radical idea, best applicable to peacebuilding missions in weak states, is to have peace operations be self-sustaining by "living off the land" (Daudelin and Seymour 2002). Peace operations could raise their own revenue by controlling key resources in the country and using revenues from their sales, seizing illegitimate assets (stolen government funds), imposing taxes and customs fees, and holding various groups directly responsible for reconstruction. Controlling resources, such as diamonds or oil, may also take away sources of financing for those who wish to continue fighting as well as provide revenue to fund the peace operation.

United Nations Security Insurance Agency A particularly innovative idea for addressing UN funding as well as security needs is the creation of an insurance system for states. The United Nations Security Insurance Agency (UNSIA) would be similar in design to insurance companies that write policies for home or auto insurance. The insurance policy would guarantee each country specific rights to UN services in the event of war or other incidents. Coverage might involve the right to preventive military actions, defense, or a peace operation deployment for a state, although the policy would be tailored individually to each state. The proposal for a UNSIA seems to presume the presence of UN standing forces that are available on short notice to respond to emergencies, although one could easily envision a modified arrangement without this component but including a commitment for standby forces from member states. The major difference between UNSIA and conventional insurance is that recipients would be given military assistance instead of cash in the event of a calamity.

Those who qualify for insurance would fund the program with their "premiums"; one presumes that there would be differential premiums based on the level of risk and the type of coverage for the state in question. Thus, as with conventional insurance policies, the new system would be self-funding, as it is assumed that not all policyholders would need to collect insurance in any given year (indeed, the system is based on only a small fraction doing so).

Single Peace Fund A second proposed program is not as dramatic as the UNSIA but is still designed to move peace operations away from the inefficient ad hoc methods of financing. The Single Peace Fund (SPF) would have a separately funded and itemized budget, independent of the overall UN budget, specifically targeted for peace operations. Establishing an annual operating budget is thought to have several advantages. First, it ensures that money for peace operations is available on short notice and so relieves organizational staff of the obligations of quickly soliciting funds for emergency operations. Second, it provides the flexibility to have funds for unanticipated operations, not merely in the short term but over the course of a year as well; it is presumed that a budget would contain such a cushion to handle new operations. Finally, maintaining a separate budget might deter the UN from raiding peace operation funds in order to pay bills in other parts of the organization (there is some evidence that the UN has chosen to fall behind on paying troop-contributing countries in favor of meeting other obligations). The net effect of an SPF would be to ensure better reaction time to crisis situations and perhaps better management, as planning, training, communications, and other duties might be consolidated rather than scattered across the organizational bureaucracy, as is currently the case.

Incorporating peace operations in national defense budgets A third new program would shift the funding of peace operations away from direct member contributions to an ad hoc fund in the direction of funding operations out of national defense budgets. Member states would have a line item in their defense budgets for peacekeeping operations or contribute a set percentage (10 percent has been suggested) of their defense budget to peace operations. States in the region of an operation might defray all the costs associated with that operation, either by paying for a specific operation directly or by contributing to a fund designed to cover all peace operations in their geographic area.

The creation of new programs, such as the UNSIA, appears severely flawed in several ways. They do not seem to guarantee that the UN and regional organizations will be free of the same problems as the current system, and they tend to create new problems that may make the financial problems of the organization worse. It is also the case with the new programs that their likelihood of adoption remains relatively low.

Despite more than fifty years' experience with peace operations, the international community still organizes, supplies, and funds those missions in a largely ad hoc and inefficient manner. Those conducted by the UN and regional organizations, by far the most common, still rely heavily on the generosity of members each time an individual operation is authorized. Although there have been some efforts to institutionalize these arrangements, the most ambitious proposals have met with resistance. Given the way that peace operations are organized, one might expect that they would encounter serious difficulties in carrying out their mandates. Yet, as the next chapter reveals, many such operations are successful, nonetheless, and the key factors influencing such success or failure are those largely outside the control of the peace operations themselves.

CHAPTER FOUR

The Success and Failure of Peace Operations

In 1988, UN peacekeeping forces were awarded the Nobel Peace Prize. On at least two other occasions, the prize was awarded to individuals and organizations (in 1957 to Lester Pearson and in 2001 to the UN/Kofi Annan, respectively) with close ties to peace operations. Awards such as these are consistent with the popular assumption that peace operations are inherently good things – who could possibly oppose a mechanism to promote peace? From a policy perspective, however, we need to develop an objective evaluation of the impacts that peace operations have. Even if that assessment is generally positive, the success of all peace operations is unlikely. Rather, success is conditioned by a series of factors, and policymakers would benefit from understanding when peace operations might be gainfully employed and when other conflict management techniques are better suited. The first step is to understand what it means for a peace operation to be successful. This may seem obvious, but remarkably few analysts employ explicit criteria in their judgments.

What Does it Mean to be Successful?

Although there are numerous studies of the success of peace operations, many with the goal of drawing lessons for future operations, less attention is given to defining what is meant by success. Most often, scholars delve into the reasons why an operation succeeded or failed without detailing how that assessment was reached. Sometimes, the operational criteria are implicit in the discussions of the alleged influences, but explicit *a priori* conceptualizations of success and operational indicators are relatively rare.

Defining the success of a peace operation is not as easy as it might seem and, accordingly, there is some disagreement among analysts over appropriate criteria. First, the question arises: success for whom? There are several sets of stakeholders in peace operations, each of which might generate different standards for success: the international or regional community, the main protagonist states or groups, the local population, and the states contributing soldiers. Although stakeholders may share some common interests (e.g., limiting violence), their other interests are not completely coterminous. The international community seeks to promote long-term stability and the preservation of human rights. The primary disputants have their own concerns, which may include controlling as much territory as possible. Stopping the fighting may be only a temporary goal, providing time for rearming and resupply. The local population may not be aligned with any combatant groups, and their primary interests might be in returning to their homes and having adequate access to food and medical care. The states contributing soldiers have the safety of their personnel as one of the most important goals.

Judgments of success measured according to the different interests above could yield very different outcomes. Indeed, success for one stakeholder could undermine success in the eyes of another. After a highly publicized loss of American soldiers, US forces in Somalia (UNITAF) took inordinate steps to limit future casualties; this came at the expense of restoring order and protecting the local population. In Bosnia, a peace force (UNPROFOR) that could not protect the local population undermined the human rights goals of the world community but actually benefited Serb forces, which were able to seize territory and "cleanse" local areas. Thus, any evaluation of peace operations should consider multiple perspectives.

Second, defining success varies according to whether one adopts a short- vs. long-term perspective. Success may be conceptualized as achievement of goals that arise during the course of a peace operation or in some time frame following the withdrawal of the force. An example is the alleviation of starvation and the improvement of medical conditions during a humanitarian operation. Thus, despite its other problems, the two UN operations in Somalia (UNOSOM I and II) can be considered successful, as food and medical aid was delivered to internally displaced Somalis. A longer-term perspective might necessitate the absence of violent conflict for several years following the operation, or in the case of Somalia the consolidation of a functioning democratic government (a condition that has not been met).

Both the long- and the short-term standpoints have utility. Nevertheless, a longer-term perspective often leads to a different assessment of an operation's success or failure. For example, various peace efforts in East Timor (e.g., UNTAET) were almost universally considered a success in the immediate aftermath and the achievement of state independence in 2002. Nevertheless, there was a reassessment of that mission and its successor, the United Nations Mission of Support in East Timor (UNMISET), when violence and instability returned in 2006, prompting the deployment of the United Nations Integrated Mission in Timor-Leste (UNMIT). Six years later, UN personnel were able to withdraw and hand control over security to East Timor police forces. Depending on when an assessment was made, conclusions about the initial operation and its successors will vary.

For most stakeholders, long-term goal achievement is paramount, but this is often the most difficult to assess. One question is how long a time frame should be considered in assessing peace operation outcomes. Given path dependency and other effects, peace operations may have consequences that extend for decades. Yet, extraordinarily long time frames make it impossible to assess ongoing and recently concluded operations. Furthermore, the longer the time period that passes between the end of the operation and the assessment, the more difficult it will be to draw causal conclusions about the impact of the operation; intervening forces are likely to have an impact as great as or greater than the peace operations on future conditions. Finally, long-term assessment is likely to be unsatisfactory for policymakers, who often cannot wait years to judge the value of an operation. Decisions on whether to continue a mission or pursue alternative means for conflict management often require some evaluation even before the peace operation is terminated. Indeed, one of the bases for deciding whether to continue or end a mission is whether the operation has successfully completed its tasks.

A third consideration is developing a baseline or standard against which to assess peacekeeping's effects. One possibility is that peace operations be judged against a situation in which no action was taken by the international community. This "better than nothing" standard, however, biases any judgments. First, decision-makers rarely choose between launching a peace operation and taking no action; a broader menu of complementary and substitutable options (e.g., economic sanctions) is available. Second, any improvement in the situation after the peace operation gets deployed is considered a success, without having regard to its cost. Thus, positive assessments are likely in most cases.

Another standard depends on comparing the conditions prior to deployment with those during and following the peace operation. This standard has the advantage of adjusting the baseline to the conflict context, as moderate levels of violence during the peace operation may be considered progress in some contexts (e.g., deployment during full-scale civil war, as in Bosnia), but backsliding in others (e.g., deployment following a ceasefire, as in the Ethiopia–Eritrea conflict). This still has the problem of regarding any improvement as successful and potentially ignoring broader and longer-term mission goals.

Other analysts suggest relating effectiveness across peace operations. Yet this generates only comparative assessments of what may be dissimilar operations and provides no absolute assessment baseline. Can one really compare a mission sent to the Congo or Sudan in the midst of heavy fighting with one that is deployed in Namibia or elsewhere that was put in place following a comprehensive peace settlement?

Regardless of mission or the phase of conflict in which the peacekeeping operation is deployed, there are some generic standards for success applicable to all missions. Perhaps the most common one is conflict abatement. All operations are supposed to discourage violent conflict (e.g., renewed war, organized crime) – a prerequisite for any other mission tasks that might be performed. Among the various indicators of progress might be the number of combatant and peace-keeper casualties, shooting incidents, or, most commonly, the number of days or months without renewed warfare.

Somewhat less common, although still prominent, is conflict containment; this involves preventing the conflict from expanding to take in additional internal actors, neighboring states, or major powers. Indicators of success for this criterion include the number of parties involved in the conflict and arms and financial flows to the combatants. Finally, many analysts assign peacekeepers the role of creating an environment suitable for conflict resolution. Yet this would seem applicable only to those operations deployed prior to a peace agreement. The presence of ongoing negotiations and actual settlement agreements could serve as benchmarks to chart progress according to this standard.

Beyond some generic standards, success is often defined according to the completion of individual tasks. Given the wide range of different missions carried out in traditional peacekeeping and peacebuilding operations, there may be standards created related to election supervision, troop withdrawal and disarmament, the creation of civil society institutions, and human rights, among many others. The starting point for most of these criteria is the mandate given the operation. In one sense this is appropriate, as a particular mission is judged only according to the task with which it was assigned. On the other hand, there are a number of drawbacks associated with using mandates to define success. First, mandates are the products of political deliberation and compromise, and the result is that they are frequently vague. There is much room for debate on the scope and detail of an operation's mission; this alone makes it difficult to assess whether the designs of the mandate have been achieved. Second, mandates may be inflexible in the face of changing conflict conditions, and thus what peacekeepers are attempting to do may no longer reflect the standards present in the mandate. Third, "mandate clarity" is regarded by some as associated with peacekeeping success, making the whole use of mandates in evaluations problematic.

A Decision Template

The evaluation of peace operations is a process, even if analysts do not consciously proceed through a series of interrelated steps. Figure 4.1, from Diehl and Druckman's (2010) work, provides a summary of these steps and their sequence. The first in the process is the identification of the primary goals of an operation, and these turn on distinctions made among

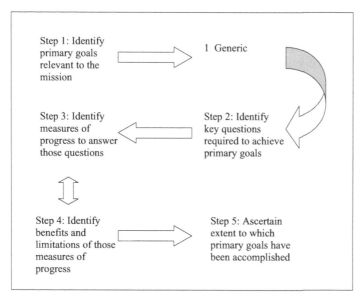

Figure 4.1 The decision template

different mission objectives. Peace operations perform a variety of missions, and therefore one must account both for the goals associated with those missions that the operation does perform and concordantly those that it does not.

Different questions, and resultant indicators, are derived from the set of initial goals. Key questions are tailored to the mission goals; that is, for each mission goal, there will be a unique evaluation question (and possibly more than one) with accompanying multiple indicators. The goals and many of the questions are determined by the mandate given the mission and its intersection with the context in which the peace operation is deployed. Answering the key questions is, in large part, how one makes a judgment about the successes or failures of the mission. Mission goals can shape the way that outcomes are evaluated. The more ambitious the goal, the less likely might the mission be regarded as being successful. For example, a mission intended to transform adversaries into allies is a greater challenge than one intended to hold a single democratic election following a peace agreement.

The precise questions in Step 2 are then answered by specifying appropriate measures of progress (Step 3). These could be quantitative or qualitative measures. They might be gained from existing data sets or reports as well as from information collected directly by personnel in the peace operation or its sponsoring agencies. This is a more difficult task because the scholarly and practitioner literatures are weaker on defining mission effectiveness. Commentary on the measures takes the form of a listing of benefits – such as "easily assessed" – and limitations – such as the "need for baseline data" (Step 4). The final step is a holistic assessment based on the individual components and evidence associated with where along a success–failure continuum an operation might fall (Step 5).

A variety of factors can militate against the force's contribution to achieving the mission's goal. International events, restrictions imposed by host states, available resources, and the vagaries of national policies are some of the factors that influence a conflict but are largely out of the peacekeepers' control. Some analysts suggest evaluating peace operations only to the extent that they control outcomes. We think that such an approach lacks validity and is mistaken. Analysts should make an evaluation of the peace operation on the dimensions specified and not confound that evaluation with determinations of how much influence peace operations had on those outcomes. That is, the measure of the outcome variable should not be confused with or determined by the purported strength of the independent variables. When an outcome assessment is made, analysts can then determine the degree to which aspects of the peace operation influenced those outcomes. To analyze outcomes that are influenced only by the peace operation presumes an *a priori* confirmation of the effects of that particular operation. This results in a biased or unrepresentative sampling of cases, probably in a positive direction. Furthermore, even hypothesized impacts are likely to be misleading, given that peace operations have many unintended effects.

There is neither the space nor the need to reprint a full range of evaluation questions, indicators, benefits, and limitations for each of the missions and associated goals of different operations; Diehl and Druckman (2010) provide extensive discussions and summary tables. Rather, we offer two illustrative examples, one each from the core and peacebuilding goals respectively: violence abatement and restoration, reconciliation, and transformation. These are given in table 4.1.

In moving from the conceptual framework to its operationalization, note first that each goal begins with more than one key evaluation question; indeed, as goals become more complex or multidimensional, the number of evaluation questions increases. This raises the possibility that peace operations might be successful on some aspects of a particular goal and not others; thus, binary judgments on peace operations are likely to be misleading. Undoubtedly, various goals are not always compatible with one another, and it is often the case that peace operations are successful at some tasks while failing at others (Martin-Brule 2012). Next, even for single evaluation questions, there are multiple indicators that can be used. This has several purposes. Many evaluation questions are multidimensional themselves and require different indicators to tap those dimensions. In addition, multiple indicators provide greater validity to the assessment, as no judgment is dependent on a single measure, which might be biased or have limitations when applied in a particular context. Finally, the data or information for certain indicators might not be available for an operation under scrutiny, and

Table 4.1 Illustrative mission goals: violence abatement and restoration, reconciliation, and transformation

Goals/objectives	Key questions	Measures of progress	Benefits	Limitations
Violence abatement (reduced violence between primary conflict combatants)			Transparent, quantifiable (all indicators below)	Strategies/intentions of actors are not revealed; validity of data for assessment of success is uncertain (all indicators below)
	Is violence (still) present?	Days/months without war (peace duration)	Comparable across missions	Major failures provide feedback too late, *post hoc* indicator
		New crises, militarized disputes, or wars	Well-developed criteria for identifying incidents, comparable across missions	Little advanced warning to allow intervention
	Have violence levels decreased?	Shooting incidents	Comparable over time	Appropriate baseline debatable; pre-violence statistics might be unavailable, do not provide insight into severity or consequences of violent acts
		Conflict-related disputant/civilian casualties	Data available	Contrasting estimates possible, must differentiate between random and mission-threatening violence
		Peacekeeper casualties	Reliable estimates, data can be gathered unobtrusively	Figures are usually low/vary little across missions, do not necessarily indicate threat to mission

Restoration, reconciliation, and transformation (changing attitudes and relationships in order to prevent a recurrence of armed conflict)	Have past crimes been addressed?	Number of war crimes trials at national or international courts	Transparent, data available	Justice might take many years; might only be mechanism to punish war losers
		Percentage of wanted war criminals arrested/ convicted	Transparent, data available	Justice might take many years; might only be mechanism to punish war losers
		Creation of truth and reconciliation commission	Transparent	Creation of the commission does not ensure that reconciliation will occur; could backfire; might preclude criminal prosecutions
	Are displaced persons being repatriated/ resettled?	Number (or percentage) of refugees repatriated/resettled	Quantifiable; estimates available	Refugees might not always want to be returned; return of refugees could reignite conflict or create schisms
	Have relations between conflicting parties changed during and after deployment?	Number/type of collaborative activities among members of the formerly conflicting groups	Observable	Difficult to discern motives (i.e., whether collaboration is strategic bargaining or genuine cooperation)
	Do institutions and culture promote peaceful conflict resolution?	Number of (and enrollment in) programs for developing conflict resolution skills	Transparent, data available	Time lag between creation of programs and appearance of program effects within society; courses may be disconnected from application/practice
		Number of professional mediation association and certified mediators	Transparent; quantifiable	Does not indicate effectiveness of mediation

therefore the multiple indicators can be substitutes for one another. It is important also to call attention to the observation that indicators can involve both quantitative data and qualitative information and come from many sources, including extant data collections, public sources, and the sponsoring agency of the peace operation, as well as what might be collected by the peace operation. For each indicator, we note its potential benefits and limitations, recognizing evaluators must weigh difficulties in information collection and measurement validity in deciding on evaluation instruments and making judgments.

There have been numerous studies of peace operation success, albeit many without explicit criteria and many not extending beyond a single operation. Nevertheless, there are some discernible patterns in whether peace operations are successful and under what conditions.

The Impact(s) of Peace Operations

Peace operations have multiple purposes, but all of them seek to ameliorate the conditions associated with a conflict. How effective are those operations? One set of research studies has sought to determine whether peace operations really result in improvement of the situation. Typically, such studies define success with simple indicators of conflict abatement, most notably at the "duration of peace" following the deployment of the operation. Yet we recognize that peace operations alone cannot halt future conflict or resolve long-standing conflicts. Accordingly, many of these studies weigh the effects of peace operations vis-à-vis other important factors and consider conflict cases with peace operations deployed as well as control groups without such operations. We look at the results of these studies, first to establish whether peace operations have a positive impact. Then we turn to a second set of studies, those that look only at peace operations, and judge what elements lead to success or failure. Although often limited, these studies reveal the different factors that condition whether peace operations have positive or negative effects, as such operations are neither uniformly desirable nor to be systematically avoided.

Peace Operations and Outcomes

To what extent do peace operations actually help to keep the peace? Many studies focus on single operations and draw conclusions about their effectiveness. Looking across these types of analyses, it is easy to find examples of successes, failures, and situations that fall in between those extremes.

Among traditional operations, most would classify the UNDOF operation on the Golan Heights as a success. Although the rivalry between Israel and Syria has continued and the two states have clashed several times in Lebanon (directly and indirectly), none of the fighting has occurred in the Golan Heights area. In contrast, the UNIFIL deployment in southern Lebanon is regularly cited as an example of a clear failure. The operation was helpless as rocket fire from Palestinian camps rained over the heads of peacekeepers into Israel, followed by Israeli retaliatory raids. Israeli invasions of Lebanon in 1982 and 2006 were also not deterred by UN peace operations. The case of UNFICYP, deployed since 1964, presents a more ambiguous case. There were a number of violent incidents in its early years, followed by the Turkish invasion in 1974 which established the autonomous Turkish Republic of North Cyprus. Since then, however, there have been few incidents, and there is general stability on the island.

Among newer peace operations, the record is equally mixed. Although not without some initial problems, the UNTAG force in Namibia is generally regarded as a good operation. It supervised the withdrawal of South Africa from the country and facilitated free and fair elections that led Namibia to become a majority-ruled, independent state. In contrast, UNAMIR in Rwanda is perhaps the most notorious failure of a peace operation. Familiar to many from the movie *Hotel Rwanda*, the mission was helpless as Hutu gangs rounded up Tutsis and systematically killed them, producing genocide of monstrous proportions, with estimates of approximately 800,000 dead. The MINUSTAH, taking over from the MIF in Haiti in 2004, was mandated to promote stability in that state, assist the transitional government, and promote democracy and human rights. There is some evidence that the situation has improved over time, but Haiti is still far from a functioning and stable democracy. Consideration of complex operations, such as the UN Operation in Côte d'Ivoire (UNOCI), reveals that even within a single operation there can be instances of both success and failure. Despite qualified success in limiting and containing violence, as well as some success in democratization, UNOCI has experienced notable failures in promoting in disarmament, demobilization, and reintegration (Bellamy and Williams, 2012).

The historical record, therefore, is one in which there are notable successes and failures among peace operations. Yet, one might question how much of the praise or blame should be attributed to the specific mission. As noted in chapter 2, peace operations are often sent to the most severe and intractable conflicts. Thus, it might be too much to expect those missions to make a significant difference in the behavior of implacable enemies. On the other hand, there are multiple factors that might contribute to the abatement and resolution of conflict, many or most of which are not under the control of the peace operation. It may be impossible to sort out precisely the exact degree of causality of a mission in its own success or failure. Indeed, a number of the correlates of success noted below are contextual and not related to the design or behavior of the mission. Still, it is possible to get beyond single-case analyses and test the impact of peace operations across different missions and controlling for other factors.

Bratt (1996) provides an assessment of UN operations through the mid-1990s and concludes that success rate is "mediocre"; only eleven of thirty-nine operations were judged as complete successes, while nearly half (nineteen) were labeled as failures. More specifically, Fortna (2008) considers whether peace operations lengthen the time for the reemergence of war, including across different types of peace operations (observer, traditional, and multidimensional peacekeeping). She studies all cases of war (after 1945), civil and interstate. A comparison is made between cases in which peace operations were deployed and those in which no peace mission was sent; the longer the peace endures, the more successful the conditions in place during that time. Overall, she finds that peace is more durable when peace operations are deployed. Fortna attributes such success to a number of factors. She contends that peacekeepers make attacks more difficult, take away the element of surprise, and raise the international costs of aggression. Among parties that desire peace, peacekeepers mitigate the security dilemma, signal mutual intentions for a peaceful resolution, and lessen the likelihood of accidents or minor engagements that could escalate. It is difficult to test these causal mechanisms directly, although the observed aggregate effects of conflict reduction are consistent with them.

Such studies establish a statistically significant relationship between peace operations and the absence of violence, which means that the effect is not due to chance. Yet, this raises the question about the substantive effects of peace operations or how much they really do improve the situation, especially vis-à-vis other factors. Depending on a variety of analyses and time periods, Fortna (2008) notes that peace operations can reduce the renewal of warfare by 30 to 95 percent – a substantial effect indeed. She controls for the more difficult or severe conflicts into which peacekeepers are sent; thus, comparisons of conflict outcomes between contexts with and without peace operations are not biased by the different initial conditions they face. Furthermore, the effect of peace operations is impressive when considering other important factors. A decisive military victory by one side in a war is perhaps the best guarantor of a long period of peace thereafter. Yet this result cannot always be assured, and, even if it could, such an outcome may carry with it a large number of casualties, human rights atrocities, and other undesirable consequences. Even if peace operations were less effective in limiting post-war violence, they are surely preferable to the impacts of an extended war. A history of conflict ("enduring rivalries") between the participants is also associated with greater chances of war renewal, indicating that intractable conflicts may be difficult to resolve and that peace operations may provide only a temporary respite.

Beyond reducing armed conflict in the area of deployment, peacekeepers also don't want to have that conflict displaced to surrounding areas, with the net effect of only relocation rather than reduction in conflict. The one preventive peace operation, UNPREDEP, was specifically designed to head off any spread of the Bosnian conflict to Macedonia. Yet, in every other case, the spread of conflict to new areas is only a secondary concern for operations relative to the main goal of maintaining stability in the area of deployment. Nevertheless, because many civil wars are fought near international borders, one risk is that violence will spread to neighboring states. Beardsley (2011) examined the potential diffusion of conflict in the presence of peacekeeping operations and in their absence. In the absence of peacekeepers, there is substantial risk that the conflict will spread to a neighboring rival state. Having peacekeepers in place significantly reduces that risk. Thus, peacekeepers reduce conflict not only where they are sent but also in neighboring states.

Fortna's analyses cover a broad time scale and many different kinds of conflict. Reflecting recent changes in peace operations, some other studies concentrate on peacebuilding operations. These consider the impact of peace operations on a broad set of outcomes beyond the limitation of violence, including whether states were able to move toward democracy as well as avoid further conflict. Doyle and Sambanis (2006) consider all civil wars that began in the period 1945–99. Looking at the aftermath of those civil wars, the authors examine whether armed conflict was renewed, whether the state moved toward democracy, and the pattern of post-war economic growth. Among the key factors examined is whether the UN deployed a peace operation or not, and these sets of cases were compared to assess the impact of such UN operations. Broadly, peacebuilding was more successful in the presence of UN peace operations than not (also confirmed by Collier, Hoeffler, and Söderbom 2006). In particular, UN peace operations were able to delay, and in some cases prevent, the renewal of violent conflict. In addition, political participation and other indicators of democratization showed positive movement. UN operations were not, however, able to stimulate economic growth. Yet this is a case in which it may be inappropriate to blame a peace operation for failure; contextual factors and other aspects of UN actions are more likely responsible.

Even with positive results, UN peace operations are not a panacea for problems and thus a guarantee for peacebuilding success. Besides citing successes in Cambodia and El Salvador, Doyle and Sambanis present some notable cases of failure, including that in Rwanda. Sisk (2008) is more cautious in assessing the democracy–peacebuilding relationships. He finds ambiguous evidence that peace must precede a successful transition to democracy and, indeed, notes that sometimes such peace efforts actually undermine the quest for stable democracy.

The potential and limitations of UN operations in the service of peacebuilding are evident in the assessment by Paris (2004). His case studies of civil conflict reveal a number of operations that promoted peace and prosperity in war-torn territories. Yet there were some clear failures as well. His key point is that the process of peacebuilding, of which peace operations are a part, is inherently "tumultuous" and conflict generating as societies undergo dramatic transformations. In this fashion, he reminds us not only of the importance of the right context for peace operations but also of the need for long-term assessment, as short-term problems may or may not signal long-term failure.

Most general studies of peace operations focus on their ability to limit armed conflict or facilitate peacebuilding activities, and the empirical findings suggest a positive, albeit imperfect, effect. Yet studies of conflict abatement or peace duration show little interest in whether a peace agreement occurs that resolves underlying issues. Similarly, analyses of peacebuilding take the existence of some kind of peace agreement as a given and are not concerned with the conditions that brought it about. Yet one standard for assessing the success of a peace operation is its ability to promote conflict resolution, not merely conflict management. Thus, another way to assess its impact is to consider its role in resolving underlying disputes.

There is considerable disagreement over whether this should even be expected of peacekeeping forces. After all, while peace operations cannot force protagonists to make concessions and sign a peace agreement, they may affect the conditions under which peace agreements are negotiated (or not). Several analyses of the so-called peacekeeping–

peacemaking relationship have tended to rely almost exclusively on a single case: Cyprus (e.g., Sambanis 1999). Cyprus may not be a representative case, in that peacekeeping forces have been there for more than five decades, and there has been no resolution of the dispute between the Greek and Turkish communities on the island; not surprisingly, when this case is referenced, the assessment is often that peace operations inhibit conflict resolution.

In perhaps the only systematic study of its kind, Greig and Diehl (2005) examine the impact of peace operations on peacemaking or the likelihood that disputants will sign a peace agreement. They looked at a range of interstate rivalries and civil wars since 1945 and concluded, first, that the presence of peacekeepers actually made direct negotiation and third-party mediation less likely, although the effect was stronger for interstate conflict than for civil wars. That is, when peace operations were deployed, the parties to the conflict were less likely to seek diplomatic solutions, and third-party mediators were less likely to make efforts at resolving the underlying conflict. Furthermore, when mediation and negotiation did occur under the auspices of a peace operation, the protagonists were less likely to reach an agreement. Peace operations often had a greater effect on these processes than any other factor examined.

Why would peace operations undermine the prospects for conflict resolution? Greig and Diehl (2005) argue that peacekeepers lessen the chance of a "hurting stalemate" by stopping the fighting. A hurting stalemate (Zartman 2000) occurs when a conflict reaches an impasse in which neither side can expect victory and both sides are bearing the costs of continuing the conflict. Hurting stalemates are conducive to parties coming to the bargaining table and reaching a settlement. By putting peace forces in place, the costs of continuing the war are mitigated or eliminated, and therefore one of the incentives to negotiate and settle is removed. The establishment of a ceasefire and the placement of peace forces also limit the flow of information about capabilities and possible settlement terms that comes from active fighting. Although potentially an immoral method of settlement, a victory by one side or another could lead to a stable, albeit imposed, outcome. A halt in the fighting prevents one side from prevailing or at least prevents battle outcomes from signaling the parties as to the likely outcome of the war; in some conceptions, the latter is sufficient for the disputants to negotiate a settlement on those terms, given that it is less costly to accept those terms at that point than continue with more protracted fighting.

The findings suggest that policymakers confronted with an ongoing conflict face a difficult dilemma, a potential tradeoff between peacekeeping and peacemaking. On the one hand, there are powerful political, strategic, and moral reasons for deploying a peacekeeping force in conflicts marked by mounting bloodshed. Cases of genocide or recurring warfare may be so extreme that they demand peace forces in order to prevent the renewal of fighting. Indeed, the prospect of peace operation deployment may be the only way to get the protagonists to agree to a ceasefire in the first place. Once deployed, peace operations may be the best mechanisms for stabilizing the situation. Yet, the intervention of peacekeepers may not only represent a temporary solution to the fighting but may also hinder conflict management efforts aimed at resolving the issues in enduring rivalries that created the conflict in the first place. This paradox works to create situations, such as that of Cyprus, in which peacekeepers are deployed for decades, but little movement toward agreement or settlement occurs. Nevertheless, this is not to diminish the positive effects that flow from ending bloodshed and allowing the local population to live as normal lives as possible. If peacekeepers fail to keep the peace effectively, however, as has been the case in southern Lebanon and in the Congo, then conflict resolution efforts by third parties or the disputants themselves may dry up. In those cases, not only has conflict resolution been negatively impacted, but there is not even the benefit of saving lives and promoting stability in the area, the primary purpose of most peace operation deployments.

The other horn of the dilemma is present if decision-makers decide to defer the deployment of peacekeeping soldiers until after a peace agreement. In one sense, it may be advantageous in the long term for conflict to continue to occur unabated without the intervention of peacekeepers in order to allow the conflict to progress to a stage in which the disputants become more amenable to settlement. Yet, such a hands-off approach is likely to be unpalatable in the most extreme cases of conflict and may carry the risk of conflict expansion, effectively compelling third parties to intervene militarily. Furthermore, decision-makers may wait for a peace agreement that never comes, as there is no guarantee that the conditions for ending a civil war will ever be manifest, at least not for many years.

The Conditions for Peace Operation Success

The research results summarized in the previous section suggest that peace operations have, on average, positive effects on conflict abatement and in promoting peacebuilding success; at the same time, there may be some negative effects as regards promoting conflict resolution. Yet none of these effects applies to all peace operations, and there are successes and failures among all different kinds of operations and across historical eras. This raises the question: what are the conditions associated with the success or failure of peace operations? Peace operation studies have frequently addressed this question directly or indirectly, largely because the answers have the greatest policy implications. Still, most of these studies look only at deployed operations, with no comparisons drawn between these and conflicts that do not experience peace operations. Nevertheless, there are a number of systematic findings and less systematic "lessons learned" or "best practices" that provide insights into when we can expect success or problems.

The conditions for peace operation success can broadly be divided into three categories. The first set of factors, "operational," includes those associated with the ways in which the peace operations are organized and executed. In effect, these factors are those that are largely within the control of the operation itself, or at least within the purview of the authorizing agency. The second set of conditions, "contextual," refers to those elements associated with the conflict. Finally, "behavioral" aspects, or the reactions of key actors, are also potentially important for the success or failure of peace operations. Below, we review how each of these sets of conditions may impact a peace operation.

Operational
Are there ways to organize a peace operation that enhance its prospects for success? In the earliest work on peacekeeping, practitioners and former military officers regularly identified a series of factors at the operational level (e.g., Skogmo 1989) that are said to promote success. These include improving the resources provided to the operation and a variety of matters associated with training and unit coordination. Many of these assertions are suspect because they are based on the biased and personal experiences of the observers as applied to unsystematic conceptions of peace operation success derived from a single mission. Such factors (e.g., elements of command, control, and communication) are important for those organizing the mission, but they are probably better understood as indicative of the elements that affect efficiency rather than

as primary determinants of its overall success. Such micro-factors should be the stuff of military manuals rather than strategic plans for policymakers. Even when some aspects are relevant in a wider sense, they are merely indicators of some broader processes; for example, problems with mandate clarity or resources are merely indicators or manifestations of the lack of consensus within the organizing coalition or major powers in the regional or international system.

A number of commentators focus on the mandate given to the peace operation, and its clarity, as a correlate of success. The argument is that operations with clearly specified tasks are more likely to accomplish their missions. As noted above, however, the mandate and its clarity are often a function of the underlying political processes (the behavior of actors, the context of deployment, and the like) and are therefore not independent factors influencing success or failure. A similar case can be made with respect to resources. Clearly, an inadequate number of troops can cause problems with a peace operation, but that raises the question of why a suboptimal number were deployed in the first place. Usually, it is largely because the authorizing agency, most often the UN and its members, has chosen for a variety of reasons not to provide what military experts would regard as an adequately sized force. Still, few if any cases of failure can be attributed solely or primarily to force size (Pushkina 2006).

As noted in chapter 2, the authorizing agency for peace operations has varied empirically, and chapter 3 suggests that certain arrangements may be superior to others. General research, however, suggests that there is no inherent advantage of the UN over regional arrangements with respect to conflict management (Boehmer, Gartzke, and Nordstrom 2004). Some regional organizations might be ill-equipped to conduct peace operations, but the tradeoff between UN and regional-sponsored operations is not necessarily determinative of success. The best that one might be able to say is that a peace operation carried out by a certain regional grouping may experience serious problems (e.g., ECOWAS), but that the alternatives are not guarantors of success and are still subject to other influences that will determine the operation's fate.

Analysis of operational factors led Heldt (2001) to conclude in his systematic assessment of peace missions in civil wars that "the variables related to peacekeeping missions are of insignificant importance and almost all of the variation in war (i.e., success) is accounted for" by other factors. Nevertheless, several recent works suggest that organizational elements are important, with the focus less on general differences across different international organizations and more on how the organizational culture and bureaucratic practices of the sponsoring agency (generally the UN) inhibit operational success. Such studies concentrate extensively on peacebuilding activities rather than on traditional operational concerns of limiting armed conflict.

Howard (2008) focuses on organizational learning in the sponsoring organization as a partial cause of success and failure in multidimensional peacekeeping operations. She defines first-level learning as

> the UN's ability to ... *gather technical information* from the field in order to develop sound analyses of problems in post-conflict society; *coordinate* international efforts such that organizational tasks are incrementally and appropriately re-prioritized; *integrate* with the post-conflict environment so that organizational responses and routines derive primarily from field-level considerations rather than higher-level political debates at headquarters; and finally *exercise leadership* in such a way that fosters the consent of the parties involved, and resolves the many small and large crises that arise in every peacekeeping operation. (2008: 328; italics in original)

First-level learning is determined, in part, by the effectiveness of the bureaucracy, emphasizing functions in the UN Secretariat rather than field actions taken by peacekeeping commanders, as was the case in early studies. Without this kind of learning, Howard (2008: 2) argues that "the operation is unable to implement its mandate or help to construct new domestic institutions that will solidify the peace." Such learning is considered to be a necessary condition for success, but she notes that the other elements – situational factors and cooperation from leading states – are also vital. Howard also discusses "second-level learning," which refers to learning across operations. Nevertheless, she notes that this often doesn't occur, and in any case this element is not subjected to the same rigorous testing across her ten case studies as is the first kind of organizational learning.

Benner and his colleagues (2011) also note the importance of organizational learning for peacekeeping effectiveness. They find a mixed record with respect to learning. On the one hand, the UN still lacks the regional expertise and many of the resources for analysis that are necessary for management and adaptation of a peace operation; this deficiency persists despite recommendations in the Brahimi Report to address these problems. Political considerations can also inhibit learning, and this can have a deleterious effect on performance. Nevertheless, political considerations can provoke learning in some cases, and the authors cite how past failures with building police institutions and gender concerns have prompted the UN to reassess its policies and institute new procedures and strategies.

In her case study of the United Nations Organization Mission in the Congo (MONUC), Autesserre (2010) blames the dominant peacebuilding culture within the UN for failures to promote conflict resolution in Congolese society. Specifically, she criticizes the UN as having an incorrect, top-down view of conflict, with an emphasis on the super-structures of regional and global sources of tension. This view led the peace operations and associated bureaucratic personnel to ignore local actors and processes in promoting conflict resolution. Such an orientation also leads peace operations to put too much emphasis on holding elections, and doing so too early, rather than on dealing first with the underlying and lingering sources of tension in society. Similar to Howard, Autesserre recognizes that additional factors, including those related to key actors, influence peace operation success, and we now turn our attention to these other elements.

Contextual or Environmental Factors

Peace operations are not deployed in a vacuum. Rather, they must deal with the circumstances of the conflict, some of which might inhibit success. As noted in chapter 2, peace operations tend to be deployed in conflicts that are more serious than average. Yet there is still considerable variation among the contexts of operations, with the key interrelated dimensions being the kind of war, the phase of operational deployment, and the geography of the conflict.

The most important distinction in conflict context is alleged to be whether the conflict is civil or interstate; of course, conflicts such as those in the Congo and southern Lebanon exhibit characteristics of both. Generally, peace operations experience more problems in conflicts that have an internal conflict component as compared to those purely between two or more states (Diehl 1994; Wesley 1997; Jett 2000). This is an especially ominous finding, in that peace operations in the post-Cold War era have increasingly shifted to civil conflict contexts.

There appear to be several explanations for the difficulties encountered by peace operations in civil wars. First, civil conflicts often involve more than two identifiable groups;

by definition, an internationalized civil war involves more than two actors. In contrast, interstate disputes have been overwhelmingly dyadic. Thus, as the number of actors in the dispute increases, so too does the likelihood that one or more of them will object to a ceasefire and the provisions for the deployment of the peace forces; they may take military action against other actors or the peacekeeping soldiers. Thus, there is more potential for "spoilers" in civil conflicts than in interstate ones. For example, the traditional peacekeeping forces (UNEF I, UNEF II, MFO) in the Sinai between Egypt and Israel had to deal with only two armies. In contrast, UNIFIL in southern Lebanon depends on the cooperation not only of the Israeli and Lebanese governments but also that of Syria, a host of Palestinian groups, Hezbollah, and various other Lebanese militias. Needless to say, support or even acquiescence from all these groups at once has been rare.

Beyond the difficulty of aggregating multiple preferences in support of a peace operation, the geographic requirements (see below) are different in a civil conflict than in an interstate one. Civil instability may mean that several groups are operating in different parts of the country. This could necessitate the peace operation covering a broader territory, opening up the possibility of more violent incidents. Furthermore, it may be impossible to demarcate a line or area, similar to an identifiable international border or ceasefire line, separating the many sides in the conflict. The ceasefire line between Ethiopia and Eritrea is much clearer than any separation between various groups in Sierra Leone. Being from the same state and often not wearing military uniforms (indeed, sometimes not being traditional military or paramilitary units at all), participants in a civil conflict are hard to identify, much less to separate, when they occupy the same geographical area. Interstate disputants can more easily be identified and separated across internationally recognized borders or militarily defined cease-fire lines.

Civil conflict may be quite dangerous to peace forces, and the situation more difficult to control. James (1994: 17) notes that, in civil conflict, "Arms are likely to be in the hands of groups who may be unskilled in their use, lack tight discipline, and probably engage in guerrilla tactics. Light arms are also likely to be kept in individual homes, and may be widely distributed." These conditions open up the peacekeepers to sniper fire and other problems, as well as making it virtually impossible to secure a given area fully. The international response to civil conflicts, or at least that of UN peace operations, has been inappropriate and has undermined effectiveness (Wesley 1997). UN planners have misread many of the situations, and the traditional peacekeeping strategies have not easily translated into the civil conflict context. The latter problem has dissipated somewhat over time as the UN and other agencies have acquired more experience in civil wars.

There are also differences between various types of civil wars. Standard distinctions are made between wars in which ethnic fragmentation is involved and those in which it is not, and in a related fashion between secessionist conflicts and those in which rebel groups seek to overthrow the government and seize control of the whole country. The evidence is mixed as to whether such distinctions affect peace operation success. Heldt (2001) notes that secessionist conflicts are no more difficult to handle than other civil conflicts. Fortna (2008) suggests that ethnic conflicts are more prone to reignite, but her results are not statistically significant, and Heldt (2001) actually argues that ethnically divided societies are less war-prone.

Regardless of the type of war or conflict into which a peace operation is thrust, there is a history between the disputants with which peacekeepers must deal. Peace operations are not magic wands that wipe away what has gone before, and therefore it may not be surprising that conflicts with a long history may place significant constraints on the success of an operation. In interstate disputes, states with a long history of militarized disputes – what have often been labeled as enduring rivalries – are more prone to renewed fighting even with the presence of peacekeepers (Fortna 2008). More severe wars (i.e., those with higher death tolls) and those that last longer also limit the prospects for lasting peace (ibid.). In each case, such conflicts heighten and harden feelings of enmity between the opposing sides. There is accordingly less inclination among the parties to grant concessions and reconcile with their enemies than if the conflicts are less serious. Furthermore, even leaders with such an inclination may be limited by public opinion and domestic political actors (e.g., military, political parties) who would find such actions unacceptable. Ironically, the conflicts in most need of peace operations are those likely to be the most difficult to resolve.

Peace operations have also been judged to be more effective in certain phases of conflict, which is closely related to the kinds of missions that they perform (Diehl 1994; Bratt 1997; McQueen 2002; Jett 2000). There has been only one operation in the pre-violence phase (the UN operation in Macedonia), and therefore no basis yet for generalizations, although some commentators (Heldt 2001) believe that the mission of conflict prevention is one well suited to peace operations.

Research indicates that peacekeepers have problems during active hostilities, the second phase of conflict. Missions during this phase of the conflict typically involve some enforcement actions. When the peacekeepers do not have the equipment, or often even the mandate, to carry out coercive actions (Boulden 2001), difficulties often arise. Thus, peace soldiers in Bosnia

(UNPROFOR) were unable to pacify many areas, and the civil wars continued largely unabated. More successful during the second conflict phase were those missions associated with humanitarian assistance. Even in Somalia (UNOSOM I and II; UNITAF), where several peace operations encountered difficulties in establishing stability, peacekeepers were able to deliver vital food and medical supplies to internally displaced people.

Peace operations are generally given credit for conflict abatement in the post-ceasefire, pre-settlement phase. Thus, traditional peacekeeping forces in the Middle East, such as UNDOF on the Golan Heights and both UNEF missions in the Sinai, have been successful in promoting stability. Yet the consensus seems to be that peace operations are most effective in a fourth conflict phase, after the disputants have signed a peace agreement (not merely a ceasefire), and the force is charged with assisting in the implementation of that agreement (Heldt 2001; Diehl 1994). Deployment in that phase gets the operation out of the peacemaking dilemma identified by Greig and Diehl (2005) and increases the likelihood of cooperation from relevant parties. Still, success in the fourth phase relates more to the ability to prevent the occurrence of war than it does to a host of other missions associated with peacebuilding.

Conflicts have been depicted in terms of the extent to which the issues are negotiable; that is, conflicts vary in terms of how much the "bargaining spaces" of the disputants overlap and therefore compromise is possible. To some extent, issues for negotiation vary by conflict phase, with the last phase involving issues of implementation, although these can be as complex and intractable as those in earlier phases if the peace agreement is vague or leaves a variety of concerns to further deliberation. Conflicts over issues of autonomy or independence, raised often in the context of civil wars, provide many examples of issues that may not be negotiable or for which the bargaining space is narrow. Even when a peace agreement is signed, issues concerning implementation threaten their durability (Stedman, Rothchild, and Cousens 2002).

The key difference between these types of issues is the extent to which disputants regard them indivisible (the terms "symbolic" or "intangible" are also used). The bargaining model assumes that issues can be divided into gradations reflecting varying degrees of compromise from initially preferred outcomes. Within the scale of gradated outcomes, a bargaining range can be identified: this is the area of the scale anchored by each party's resistance point from which no further concessions are possible. Some bargaining theorists claim that few issues take on an "all-or-none" form and are therefore non-negotiable (e.g., Fearon 1995). This is because side payments or linkages to other issues allow parties to compensate each other for perceived losses on difficult issues. Yet, it is also the case that many causes have considerable emotional appeal – particularly those linked to ethnic conflict – making compromise difficult for those who identify with them (e.g., Brubaker 1996). Certain issues, especially territorial ones, have perceived value based on long-standing religious, historical, or ethnic connections (e.g., Jerusalem or Kosovo). It may be that cost–benefit considerations are entertained with regard to the choice between fighting and negotiating, as discussed in the literature on hurting stalemates (Zartman 2000). Negotiation is not viewed as an option "if the value to one (or more) of the parties of partial control of the stakes is low" (Wood 2003: 250–1).

Intractable issues can signal to the peace operation that a long-term deployment, as is the case in Cyprus and the Golan Heights, is likely, with all the attendant costs and risks. This may be broken only if a mutually enticing opportunity arises, turning points in the negotiation are stimulated, or issues are reframed. It is possible for peace operations to have some minor effect on these processes, although they are more likely the responsibility of diplomatic initiatives that accompany the operations. Even when successful negotiation has occurred, recurrent peace operations are more likely when agreements reconcile past grievances but do not provide resolutions that are blueprints for the future, as was the case in Haiti.

Another contextual factor concerns the geographic configuration of the conflict and the accompanying peace operation deployment (Diehl 1994). Peace missions are most successful when deployed so as to detect ceasefire violations and monitor compliance with other mandates adequately. Often this is well beyond the ability of the operation. If an operation is charged with supervising an election (as was the case with UNTAC in Cambodia) or with monitoring the aftermath of a broad civil war (as was the case with MONUC in the Congo), this may mean being responsible for an entire country. Even with an extremely large peace force, this is on the whole impractical; for example, the Congo covers 2,267,599 square kilometers and shares borders with nine other states as well as having a coastal area. A limited transportation system further complicates the ability of an international force to monitor activities there.

Large size is not the only barrier to effective peace missions. Topography must also be conducive to monitoring. An open terrain and a lightly populated area are favorable to the detection of improper activity by disputants. If the parties believe that they can get away with violations, then sniper fire, smuggling, and other actions will be more likely to occur. Accordingly, the open desert terrain of the Sinai (where MFO operates) or the sparsely populated areas of the Golan Heights (where UNDOF functions) seem ideal geographically for detecting movement. In contrast, the dense jungles of the Congo or the high-traffic area of southern Lebanon (where UNIFIL operates) make it difficult to monitor activities.

Peace operations must also be relatively invulnerable to attack themselves and, in a related manner, be able to separate combatants. Opponents of peace missions may be tempted to attack the peacekeepers if doing so would weaken the resolve of the sponsoring agency or donating states to the mission as a whole. Although peace soldiers do not always get to choose their deployment space, it is clear that low-lying areas surrounded by hills (perfect for rocket and other attacks) were very harmful to MNF soldiers in Lebanon during the early 1980s. Equally important, disputants must be prevented from direct engagement with one another. This is almost impossible in certain contexts. Urban environments, whether in Beirut, Kigali, or Mogadishu, are very difficult to monitor because of the large and heterogeneous populations moving about the area. The narrow Green Line in Beirut, separating Christian and Muslim communities, is far from the ideal arrangement. An identifiable international border is clearly preferred. Yet civil wars often have no identifiable ceasefire lines. UN forces in Lebanon and outside Srebrenica in Bosnia cannot stop rocket attacks that sail over their heads. How does a peacekeeping force in Sierra Leone (UNOMSIL) keep track of a variety of militia groups? Furthermore, many peacebuilding missions are predicated on promoting the interaction of formerly hostile groups; this may be necessary, but it also increases the risk that spoilers of the peace process will launch attacks.

Some Special Concerns for Peacebuilding
For peacebuilding operations, the contextual factors that promote success are not necessarily the same as those described above as inhibiting the renewal of violence. Reduced levels of hostility, as with more traditional peace operations, assist

peacebuilding missions. Yet the factors promoting success in tasks beyond violence limitation can be difficult to discern; peacebuilding is a long-term process, and it is difficult to identify correlates of success for a process that is still incomplete in most cases.

Paris (2004) is critical of the way in which peacebuilding strategies have been implemented. He decries the world community's attempts to build democracy and stability too quickly and without adequate resources. He also thinks that the domestic institutions need to be properly strengthened before peacebuilding can succeed. The war-proneness of democratizing states (Mansfield and Snyder 2005) is a further condition that seems to complicate any attempts at peacebuilding. Paris argues that the right sequencing of conditions is key for success, and that peacebuilding missions can have an impact on these, based on the choice of appropriate strategies. He advocates promoting economic policies that moderate rather than exacerbate conflicts and ensuring that the state has effective security institutions and competent bureaucracies. Supplementing these are civil society organizations that can unite different parts of society and mitigate factors that promote conflict. These elements, whether they are already present or need to be built, are essential in the short term and will in any case pay dividends in the long term. Similarly, Doyle and Sambanis (2006) contend that local capacity, defined in terms of local economic health and resources, is also strongly related to success. The state to which a peacebuilding mission is sent can be compared to a sick patient. Armed conflict and its aftermath are one set of pathologies, but if the patient is also wracked by other diseases, then recovery is going to be difficult. A healthy economy and a functioning governance system pave the way for other peacebuilding activities; the society is then ready for additional treatments carried out by other actors and/or facilitated by the peace operation.

Increasing levels of political participation have not necessarily expanded economic growth, suggesting that the latter may be a higher first priority than the former.

Notably, Paris and others do not see democratization as the panacea or the first step in peacebuilding activities. Indeed, for Doyle and Sambanis and others, democratization is a measuring stick rather than a causal agent for success. Paris cautions against democratic elections being conducted too soon in the peacebuilding process, a point echoed by Autesserre (2010). There needs to be some opportunity for reconciliation and stability. Plans for elections and governing systems must also be carefully chosen. Doyle and Sambanis note that ethnically divided societies already pose a difficult context for peacebuilding. If electoral rules (e.g., plurality vs. majority vote requirements) reward hate speech and encourage the rise of political parties and movements that emphasize ethnic differences, the long-term prospects for peace are not good. IFOR efforts in Bosnia and Croatia have helped limit the renewal of civil war, but broader peacebuilding (e.g., such as the repatriation of refugees) has been stifled by elections that have handed power to ethnically polarized parties.

Another key element of the conflict environment is the degree to which basic government services (e.g., water, electricity) are provided in the deployment and related areas. The supply of such services will, in part, define the goals and scope of the mission at the outset. That is, if such services are not being provided or exist at inadequate levels, then the mandate and responsibilities of the mission are likely to be expanded; time and the material resources required will be greater as well. The status of those services will also influence the success of the operation – as services improve or already exist at adequate levels, the peace operation will be able to promote stability and move ahead with other aspects of the mission.

In failed states and in areas that have experienced significant destruction from conflict, the provision of basic services such as water, electricity, medical care, and fire protection may have been disrupted. A peace operation will need to devise plans to narrow the gap between the desired level of services and the current provision, and this may involve allocating its own resources and aligning with other actors (e.g., local authorities, NGOs) to ensure delivery. Nevertheless, these are tasks over which peace operations have significant control and whose conditions can be ameliorated in the short run. As the situation improves, the peace operation must guard against retrenchment, as spoilers can target the delivery of such services as a way of undermining the mission and promoting instability. For example, a hostile party might target the electricity grid as a way of undermining a wide range of different activities in society.

Even if basic services are operational, there must be a concern with which actors are providing those services. If the host government is the entity, then the peace operation's role is more limited. If NGOs (e.g., Doctors without Borders) or private entities are the providers, there may need to be some transitional arrangements in which local authorities eventually assume responsibility. Most dangerous might be provision by local militias or political groups. Although having those services is desirable, there is the risk that such actors may establish parallel and alternative government structures that threaten long-term stability and national government authority. Such services may also be withheld at times for political purposes. Black market provision of services and products, such as fuel, are sometimes more desirable than their total absence, but this creates alternate authorities, encourages criminal activity and corruption, and may hamper the reestablishment of legitimate service provision in the future.

Along with cooperation and the provision of services, a key element of a functioning society is its infrastructure –

namely, the condition of the roads, ports, pipelines, electricity grids, and communication systems in the host state. Again, if these are degraded, it will become part of the peace operation's responsibilities to improve them, either alone or with the assistance of local authorities and international development actors (e.g., the World Bank, NGOs); in the short and medium term, such conditions are not malleable. Problems with infrastructure also complicate the ability of the peace operation to complete other mission tasks. For example, poor or non-existent roads (as in the Congo) make it nearly impossible to get food and medical supplies to refugees or displaced populations.

As peace operations begin to rebuild infrastructure, there should be a cascading effect, *ceteris paribus*, with success. Improved infrastructure necessitates fewer operational resources while facilitating the achievement of many other goals of the operation. In addition, logistics are facilitated when the host country has functioning airports, ports, and roadways, and increased economic development is more likely under those conditions, as is recovery from violent conflict.

A further environmental condition concerns natural resources, largely a fixed condition that will be unaffected by the peace operation. The first consideration is the number and type of natural resources present in the host state. Important natural resources most obviously include oil and diamonds, but precious metals, natural gas, timber, and other resources are relevant as well. A well-endowed host state is one in which there is a variety of valuable resources that are in abundant supply.

A second consideration is which actors control the access to and distribution of those resources. Are those resources in the hands of legitimate government authorities or are they under the control of rebel groups, armed militias, or third-party interveners? If the resources are under the control of government authorities, they can provide a revenue stream for those authorities and so the basis for economic recovery and development, although corruption is a risk as well. Still, if those resources or their distribution are vulnerable (e.g., natural gas pipelines in Afghanistan or oil-processing facilities in Iraq), then the peace operation has a security problem that must be addressed both in the short term and in the long term when control is turned over to local forces.

Control of natural resources by opposition forces or outsiders is especially problematic for a peace operation. Such groups will resist the reestablishment of government control. Marketing of those resources may also be used to fund violent activities, with revenues used to purchase weapons and bribe local officials. Particularly suitable for these purposes are those resources that are "lootable" – that is, capable of being easily transported and marketed elsewhere, which tends to lengthen the duration of armed hostilities, particularly in non-separatist conflicts. Most illustrative of these effects was the presence of diamonds in the Congo, which served to prolong the violence, promoted corruption, and encouraged outside military intervention.

Another factor impacting local capacity is the economic situation in the country (countries) of deployment. This is generally significant for two different processes. First, economic conditions will influence the likelihood of conflict renewal and escalation, as looting, criminal activity, and group-based grievance are associated with higher levels of violence. Second, the state of the economy will help define the depth and scope of tasks assigned to peace operations as well as the duration of the mission.

Peace operations have little ability to transform quickly the economic conditions in their area of deployment. Furthermore, such operations are not generally deployed to states or territories with advanced economies. Neither do they find themselves deployed where robust economic activity is common. Violent conflict of the type that would precipitate the intervention of a peace operation does not occur in the wealthiest societies. Thus, peace operations will generally find themselves in poorer states, and problems will vary more by degree than in kind.

The recovery capacity of states is greater under conditions of economic health. One can assume that the violent conflict that precipitated the peace operation resulted in some economic dislocation and problems. At the extreme, this could involve the destruction of infrastructure or industry, the disruption of agriculture, and the dislocation of large segments of the population; the conflict in Darfur is clearly indicative of the latter two. In such circumstances, there are tremendous pressures on the peace operations, as their ability to restore stability is compromised.

Larger, more diversified economies have greater recovery capacity than those centered on a single commodity or industry. Diversification also suggests a greater capacity to meet the varied needs of the population. Whether it is coordinating relief supplies or providing security for various peacebuilding exercises, the narrower the range and scope of duties, the more friendly the environment for the peace operation. Unhealthy economies will also likely necessitate more sustained peace operations.

The distribution of wealth in a society is another contextual factor. Those with widely disparate income distributions are potentially the most problematic for peace operations. Wealth concentrated in one segment of these societies will signify greater poverty in contrast to a much smaller number of economic elites. To the extent that such a distribution reinforces the ethnic or other cleavages described below, the potential for conflict escalation and renewal is exacerbated. Greater poverty and the potential for grievance derived from that puts the impetus on peace operations to provide stability and facilitate peacebuilding tasks sooner. Early deployment and effective coordination on the ground cannot wait months, lest problems fester and conflicts reignite.

The capacity for sustainability and recovery is also conditioned by the opportunities for growth present in the economy. An asymmetrical trade balance in the direction of imports creates a dependency on the part of the host territory and probably a need for additional aid to the local population. Similarly, large-scale debt means that internal resources are directed outward rather than having fungible value. As with other features of local capacity, any elements that diminish resources that can be directed inward might expand the scope of peace operation duties and lengthen deployment times. These conditions are not easily redressed in the short term.

Peace operations have to deal with whatever local population exists in the area of deployment as well as any cleavages between them; although some amelioration is possible over time, this element is largely fixed in the short term. Gurr, Woodward, and Marshall (2005) found that the second most important driver of ethnic wars was the combination of population size and diversity. Ethnic wars were five to eight times more likely to occur in larger countries with medium to high ethnic diversity; Iraq provides the most well-known contemporaneous example. State-led discrimination policies were the most important influence on ethnic wars. Large homogeneous countries, such as Turkey, or small, heterogeneous countries, such as Peru, are less prone to dangerous internal conflict. Thus, ethnically divided societies provide the greatest challenges for peace operations, regardless of mission purpose (violence avoidance, human rights protection, humanitarian assistance).

These population dimensions become fault lines for conflict when members use certain categories, such as ethnicity

and religion, as a rationale for political dissent. It is important for peacekeepers to know which category elicits strong
identifications within the population and the conditions that
increase the salience of that category as a rallying point for
political action. With regard to the former, a particular dimension, such as religion, can become attached to other lines of
division, such as social class or political ideology, serving to
polarize the groups further and escalate the conflict. When
several dimensions overlap or become mutually reinforcing,
the conflict moves increasingly in the zero-sum direction,
with diminished prospects for settlement or rebuilding. A
challenge for peace operations is to discourage disputing parties from expanding the definition of the conflict by adding
dimensions of difference or fault lines while encouraging
them to use other dimensions as shared identities.

The peace operation has to deal with the cleavages not only
between indigenous groups but also between itself and the
local population (Pouligny 2006). Some of this is inherent, as
in the clash of military and civilian cultures. Yet there may be
significant differences between the cultures and norms of the
peacekeepers (who themselves vary) and the local behaviors.
For example, the reciprocity norm may be standard for those
in peace operations but foreign to those from hierarchical
societies; thus, ceasefire negotiations or conflict management
at the micro-level predicated on this norm may be unsuccessful. Fortunately, some of the culture clash between the
peacekeepers and the local population can be mitigated by
training, although it is not clear whether this can be achieved
at all levels of the operation and across different national troop
contributors.

Finally, the human capital of the local population, specifically the distribution of skills particularly with regard to the
development and use of technologies, will condition the recovery potential of the society. Yet the distribution of these skills

will also mediate or exacerbate cleavage-based conflict. The more evenly skills are spread through a population, the more likely that opposition groups will possess skills that enhance their effectiveness. More effective opposition groups intensify the conflict.

Behavioral Factors

Most of the other factors identified by analysts have concerned the behavior of actors in the conflict – those directly involved as well as third parties. There is the broad generalization that the greater the number of different actors involved in a conflict, the more difficult it will be to achieve success (Diehl 1994; Doyle and Sambanis 2006). As the number of disputants increases, it becomes harder for any settlement or even a ceasefire agreement to be satisfactory to all parties. Furthermore, there is increasing opportunity for any one party to undermine the operation, for example, by refusing cooperation with state-building programs or, more seriously, by choosing to renew violence as a strategy to achieve goals. Thus, highly complex civil wars are the most difficult to resolve. In the Congo, there were numerous factions and direct military intervention by Rwanda, Uganda, Zimbabwe, and several other states, making the cooperation of numerous parties a prerequisite to deploying a peace operation and having it carry out its mandate.

The cooperation of the primary disputants (McQueen 2002; Bratt 1997; Jett 2000; Pushkina 2006) in traditional operations is thought to be most critical for the success of peace operations. Yet such claims run the risk of a tautology: if success is defined by a lack of violence by the disputants, then lack of violence by the disputants cannot be considered a causal factor. Existing research has not clearly specified when and why disputants would choose to abandon a ceasefire and undermine peace operations. One might speculate that, as the peace operation evolves, one or more of the disputants may be disadvantaged by the maintenance of the status quo in a traditional mission or by elections and changes in society during a peacebuilding one. At that stage, the interests of such parties will no longer be to support the operation but rather to renew violence. In southern Lebanon, following the kidnapping of an Israeli soldier in 2006, Israel launched attacks on Hezbollah strongholds and beyond; such attacks included those against UNIFIL, with conflicting accounts as to whether this was intended or not. Largely successful elections in Angola in 1992 led to a renewal of violence only when the losers in the election, forces loyal to Jonas Savimbi and his UNITA movement, reignited the civil war thereafter.

Beyond the primary disputants, most relevant are the actions of neighboring states (Pushkina 2006) or interested major powers (Bratt 1997). Third-party states can influence the success of a peace operation in several ways (Urquhart 1983). Most obviously, they can directly intervene militarily in a conflict, causing a renewal of the fighting or jeopardizing the safety and mission of the operation. This was the case in the Congo, as several states in the region joined the fighting in support of different armed groups and in pursuit of securing resources such as diamonds. More subtly, they might supply arms and other assistance to one of the disputants (or to a subnational actor – see below) that serves to undermine the peace force's ability to limit violence. Alleged Syrian and Iranian supply of weapons and money to Hezbollah has emboldened the latter to create more instability in Lebanon and to break the fragile peace with Israel on numerous occasions. Support from the former Yugoslavia provided to fellow Serbs had the same effect in the Bosnia civil war. Third parties might also bring diplomatic pressure to bear on one of the actors, such that the actor is more or less disposed to support the presence of the peace operation (Bratt 1997; Jett 2000; Diehl 1994).

In addition, third-party states might have an indirect influence on the peace operation by virtue of their relationship to the primary disputants in other contexts. Conflict between a third-party state and one of the disputants over issues related or unrelated to the conflict in question can heighten tension in the area. The new conflict could spill over and poison the cease-fire between the primary disputants. Most dangerous would be a situation in which a primary disputant is aligned with a third-party state that becomes involved in a militarized conflict with the other primary disputant. In that case, the primary disputants are often dragged into renewed conflict by virtue of competing alignment patterns. Third parties have the potential to play either a positive or a negative role in the performance of peace operations. One suspects, however, that the latter is more likely. There are potentially more ways to complicate a peace operation than to assist it. Furthermore, a third-party state that supports a peace operation will likely stay out of the conflict, whereas in opposition it will tend to take a more active role.

The exception may be the major power states, especially the remaining superpower, the United States (Bratt 1997; McQueen 2002; Howard 2008). Major powers have the military capacity and political influence to prod recalcitrant disputants to cooperate with the peace force. Yet, for most peace missions, that major power must act impartially even if it is aligned with one of the protagonists. Major powers can also play an important supplemental role, providing critical political support within the organizing agency and contributing money, logistical support, and other forms of help to the peace operation. In particular, major powers are the key players in leading international organizations, such as the International Monetary Fund and the World Bank, which will be critical in providing assistance to states during later phases of peacebuilding operations. Without the support of leading states, such assistance is not likely to be forthcoming.

Third-party states are not the only relevant actors, as many operational deployments are subject to the actions of subnational actors (e.g., see Norton 1991). These include ethnic groups, competing political movements, terrorist organizations, and NGOs. The behavior of these groups may be especially important when peace forces are thrust into areas of internal instability (Diehl 1994; Bratt 1997; Jett 2000). In some cases, subnational actors may actually control larger geographic areas than the recognized government. Unlike third-party states, however, subnational actors affect peace operations primarily by direct actions of support or opposition. For example, the Young Patriots group started riots in Côte d'Ivoire in 2006, targeting UN personnel and forcing the operation (UNOCI) to relocate personnel and staff away from the affected areas. Similarly, seven Spanish peacekeepers associated with UNIFIL were killed by a car bomb attributed to a splinter Palestinian Islamist group. Thus, the cooperation of subnational groups can be crucial in fostering a minimum level of violence in the area of deployment.

In peacebuilding operations that occur in the post-settlement phase, the success of any operation, especially a peacebuilding mission, is somewhat dependent on the degree to which it can draw upon the resources, capacity, and support of key actors in the host state (Doyle and Sambanis 2006; Paris 2004). If the host government is strong and fully functional, it is likely that a peacebuilding operation will not be necessary; peacebuilding operations are designed, in part, to strengthen local governance. Nevertheless, the more local governance capacity is present, the shorter becomes the distance to goal achievement and the easier the road to travel to reach that goal. Conversely, less local governance capacity will both necessitate an expansion in the number and scope of the tasks of the peace operation and complicate its ability to achieve them. Nevertheless, it may be difficult to measure and assess local capacity, and this must include civilian as well as governmental components (Call and Cousens 2008).

Permissiveness/consent refers to the degree to which local groups and authorities cooperate and support the peace operation; military officials often refer to this as the "permissiveness" of the environment, whereas others designate this as the degree of consent. Above, we discussed the importance of cooperation from the primary disputants, often with respect to preserving a ceasefire. Here peace operations must be concerned with the degree to which key decision-makers or strategic actors support the achievement of certain tasks, such as reestablishing local security services or distributing humanitarian assistance. The focus must move beyond state-level capacities and incorporate localized assessments as well (Manning 2003).

If local groups and authorities cooperate in various peace activities, there are several benefits to the operation. First, some local resources (e.g., transportation, personnel) might be leveraged to complete tasks, thereby lessening the burden on the peace operation agency and/or freeing up resources for allocation to other tasks. Second, cooperation in peace operation activities creates "ownership" on the part of local authorities and the population. This makes it more likely that efforts will be regarded as legitimate and therefore sustainable in the long run after the peacekeepers are withdrawn.

The corresponding problems and risks from lack of cooperation are probably greater than any benefits accrued from cooperation. Local groups or officials can undermine or even block peacebuilding efforts. For example, rebuilding infrastructure often requires getting the necessary permits from local authorities. A water treatment plant might easily be sabotaged by a group opposed to assisting a rival ethnic group or clan. In any peacebuilding activity, the goal is ultimately to turn operations over to local authorities. If they are unwilling to assume responsibilities or are hostile to them, the prospects for long-term success are slim.

Why might local officials or groups oppose peacebuilding efforts? The peace operation may undermine local authorities in several ways. Reestablishing order with regular security forces might decrease the power of local militias as well as corruption opportunities that benefit local leaders. Other peace activities may serve to strengthen rival political or ethnic factions or groups.

The cooperation of government authorities in the host state is of limited value unless they exercise effective jurisdiction over the area of deployment and related regions. In looking at government penetration and control, there are several important dimensions. First and foremost, however, is the degree to which the government, or quasi-government structure, maintains security control over given areas. The possible scenarios range from an environment in which the government has full control and the situation is stable (unlikely) to the circumstance of a failed state, in which no central or perhaps any kind of authority exists. In between may be situations in which the government control or penetration is weak or in which stability varies substantially across towns, cities, and regions. This can be redressed to some degree by peace operation policies but only in the long term and perhaps only with success in other parts of its mission, such as promoting reconciliation between disputants.

Unless authorities can maintain law and order in the area of deployment or other areas of concern, the peace operation will have great difficulty in carrying out various peacebuilding duties. For example, humanitarian assistance in the form of medical care might be impossible because access is blocked to unstable areas – exactly those with the greatest demand for such services. Even with access, the breakdown of law and order could lead to diminishing assistance as theft and bribes shrink available resources for threatened populations. Criminality also further weakens government capacity, as black market and other activity deprives institutions of tax revenues (Nitzschke and Studdard 2005). Indeed, it is likely that the peace operation will need to pacify areas and establish law and order for an extended period of time if the government is incapable of doing this. Added to the list of duties will be the training, supply, and ultimately support of new local police authorities so that the peacekeepers can finally withdraw and turn over security duties to a functioning local army or police force.

The lack of government control also has some pernicious effects on the operation. Beyond spending resources for security, local support and cooperation for the peace force could be limited, as there is significant risk to parts of the population willing to support mission goals. The resumption of normal activities is barred in some areas, putting greater burdens on the peace force to provide services. Finally, support for the peace operation will likely decline if it is unsuccessful in restoring law and order.

Overall, the key concerns with respect to third-party and subnational group cooperation are (1) their preferences and interests and (2) the resources they command (Diehl 2000). If the peace operation does not serve the interests of third parties, opposition to the force is likely to be generated. Yet this opposition alone is not sufficient to jeopardize success. These parties must have significant resources that could be brought to bear against the mission. Such resources include political influence with key actors and the local population in the area of deployment. The ability to intervene militarily or supply weaponry to those opposed to the operation may also be critical.

CHAPTER FIVE

Ten Challenges for Future Peace Operations

The founders of the League of Nations and the United Nations would no doubt be quite surprised by modern peace operations. They expected that either diplomatic and legal means of conflict resolution or more coercive collective security operations would be the primary mechanisms to ensure international peace and security. Furthermore, few if any of them saw international military personnel playing active roles in the internal social and economic transformations of states, elements now central to peacebuilding.

Even as peace operations evolved, a number of unexpected yet significant changes occurred. Although there were several observation missions previously, the creation of the first traditional peacekeeping mission in 1956 was a dramatic break from the past, and one in response to the unique circumstances of the Suez Crisis. Yet this mission would serve as a model for peace operations for many years to come. In the 1970s, few new peacekeeping operations were created, and some analysts proclaimed this approach to peace to be an anachronism for dealing with threats to international security as the Cold War matured. The end of the Cold War took most policymakers and scholars by surprise, and the revival of peacekeeping and its evolution into peacebuilding led some to overestimate the role that peace operations would play in an alleged "new world order." Such exuberance was quickly quashed with peacekeeping failures in Somalia and Rwanda. The expectation that peace operations would decline, however, was incorrect, as the UN and regional organizations alike expanded their activities, as did multinational groupings.

Predictions about peace operations have been notoriously inaccurate. The frequency and configuration of such operations have also been sensitive to major political events in the international system, which are not always accurately forecast. Thus, it is with some trepidation that we conclude this book with a look to the future of peace operations. So much will depend on changing political events and the success or failure of existing peace operations. Nevertheless, regardless of what is unforeseen, there are a number of challenges that the international community must face with respect to peace operations. How these challenges are handled will go a long way toward determining whether peace operations are a central part of promoting peace and security or whether they will appear in the list of largely discarded approaches, such as collective security.

Below are ten major challenges facing peace operations in the near and medium-range future. For each of these challenges, we give an overview or description of what is involved, the implications for peace operations, and selected policy choices that might be made to address those challenges. We also note that most contain certain dilemmas that make addressing them more complicated and often more difficult to address.

The challenges facing peace operations are classified below according to their origins. Environmental challenges are the kinds of conflicts and broader systemic issues that present peace operations with problems. Political challenges are those that involve the decisions and consequences associated with the authorization, supply, and conduct of peace operations. That is, peace operations are subject to the interests of member states (be it the UN, a regional organization, or a multinational coalition). Capacity challenges deal with the mismatch between what peace operations need to do in order to be effective and their present organizational and resource capabilities. There are also overarching challenges that do not fall easily into any one category. One is occasioned by unintended consequences of peace operations, including those related to the local economy, human rights, and criminal activity. The book concludes with the overarching challenge of the "failure of political will" – in some sense the challenge that underlies all problems, past and future, for peace operations. None of the challenges is mutually exclusive, and indeed many are so interrelated that addressing one may be a prerequisite to dealing effectively with another.

Environmental

The Changing Contexts of War
Peace operations are somewhat sensitive to the "demand" side of the equation – namely, the conflicts in which they will be asked to intervene. During the Cold War, these were primarily interstate conflicts. The notable shift toward civil wars occurred in the 1990s and continued in the new century. In the short and medium term, there is reason to believe that this pattern will persist. At the same time, new variations of civil conflicts are emerging – more specifically, in failed states and those territories undergoing political transitions, whether to independence or to functioning democracies. In either case, not only are peace operations dealing with internal actors in disputes, but the newer contexts also involve a breakdown or lack of government structures on which to support the operations and promote long-term peace. Indeed, peace operations are increasingly asked to fill those gaps and rebuild the necessary institutions.

Peace operations face significant problems in meeting these threats to international peace and security. As indicated in the last chapter, civil conflicts are associated with a lower rate of success. Civil conflicts often have a greater number of relevant actors, a broader geographic area to cover, and a difficult context for monitoring behavior. Terrorist attacks may jeopardize local stability and threaten the safety of the peace force. In addition, the breakdown of civil society and institutions all but necessitates more multidimensional peacebuilding operations, with a range of different missions and greater coordination among NGOs and international agencies. The net effect is likely to be operations that require more personnel, greater expense, and longer-term commitments.

What are the choices available to the international community in meeting these challenges? One option is to conduct security "triage" and opt to send peace operations to a limited set of conflicts. Here it may be that global and regional organizations choose only those conflicts in which the chances of success are better. Conflicts that are particularly difficult may be ignored, or efforts may be directed to seal them off from the rest of the world. Note that the EU has agreed to provide peacekeepers to Chad to protect refugees fleeing from Darfur, even as peace operations in the latter are inadequate. There are certainly moral dilemmas that arise from such a strategy, as large numbers of casualties and even genocide are possible.

The international community may also decide to expand its commitment to peace operations, attempting to deal with all major conflicts encountered. This is unlikely to be handled by any one agency, with coordinated efforts by global and regional organizations, and even multinational groupings, being necessary to meet the demand. The number of ongoing peace operations has grown substantially over the last decade, so the idea of further expansion is not out of the question. Still, it would require more resources and perhaps revised peacebuilding strategies to meet the challenge of failed states or to sustain missions in transformative societies.

Not all responses to the challenges of conflict context need to be reactive. Attempts might be made to lessen the need for peacebuilding operations or at least to modify the contexts in which they are deployed. Such actions might include greater use of preventive deployments of peacekeepers to head off state collapse or mitigate the political and humanitarian disasters that result. Similarly, enhanced diplomatic efforts might precipitate plans with better cooperation from affected parties and ones executed earlier in the reconstructive processes, so that, even if they were to be deployed, the prospects for the success and early withdrawal of peace operations would be improved.

New Missions
The end of the Cold War and the development of peacebuilding led peace operations to assume a wide range of duties beyond that of interposition. This had significant implications for when and where peace operations were deployed. There are certain tasks for which peace operations are better suited; but they are still called on to solve many problems regardless, especially as other operational alternatives in the security realm are absent. Peace operations have already been suggested for many new missions. One could see such operations assuming transitional authority in Palestine, in failed states, or in post-conflict countries around the globe. The UN has performed this function before, but the scope and duration of such missions would be new, and very much so for regional organizations. Further from present international norms would be peace operations deployed to deal with widespread human rights abuses, short of genocide, or environmental disasters, which generate significant humanitarian, economic, and conflict problem potential. National militaries are already used in natural disasters, so it is not much of a step to imagine peace soldiers taking on similar roles.

One of the dilemmas faced by sending institutions is to figure out the malleability of the mandate for peace operations. Political missions and naval peacekeeping are the latest activities added under the umbrella of peace operations. In the last decade, there has been a significant increase in the number of political missions headed by the UN Department of Political Affairs (twelve such missions as of 2013). Most political missions do not have any military component, but they are considered peace operations because they conduct either preventive diplomacy or peacebuilding activities at different conflict phases. Other political missions are not considered peace operations, as they serve the role of coordinating peace processes in a specific country (Lebanon) or region (Central Asia and the Middle East). A better understanding of the links between political missions and peace operations is needed. They all undertake conflict management in one form or another, but they have different, often overlapping, responsibilities.

A second dilemma is in respect to naval peacekeeping, and especially counter-piracy activities. The incidents of piracy have increased since the end of the Cold War, with frequent attacks occurring in several hotspots: Southeast Asia, the Strait of Malacca, the Indian Ocean, and the Gulf of Guinea. The United Nations has been paying more attention to these incidents, especially as they link to conflicts on land. Piracy has become a threat to international peace and security that peacekeepers are already asked to address, as seen in the operations by the EU and NATO off the coast of Somalia. A number of scholars (de Oliveira 2012; Bueger, Stockbruegger, and Werthes 2011) argue that peacebuilding approaches should be integral to any effective counter-piracy strategy. The naval peacekeeping's focus on "good order at sea" should be replaced by an understanding of the land-based structural conflicts that underline the problems at sea. The Somali pirates became pirates because of a devastating civil war, but also because of the decrease in the fishing stocks upon which large coastal communities depended for their daily income. An integrated sea–land approach seems to be the aim of the EU peace operation EUCAP Nestor, linking its military counter-piracy operation (EU NAVFOR) to development and security assistance components in the Horn of Africa.

The assumption of new missions, especially those that deviate substantially from current tasks, will necessarily involve different skill sets and possibly organizational arrangements; for example, Bratt (2002) suggests that peacekeepers could play an important role in fighting AIDS in Africa. New missions are also likely to represent a range of contexts, not the least of which will involve variation on host-state consent. Involvement by other agencies and NGOs would seem to be paramount in many new missions; few new missions envisioned are purely military ones in which soldiers are the exclusive personnel required.

Of course, the international community could decide to resist new missions or choose strategies not involving peace operations to address them. It may be that new strategies and institutions are created to meet these challenges, much as peacekeeping and peacebuilding evolved out of such needs. Yet, more likely, these new missions will necessitate some changes for peace operations. One option is the development of specialized troops (even under the present ad hoc system of provision), trained and deployed for only certain kinds of missions. Heretofore, peacekeepers have intervened in many different kinds of conflicts, based on the assumption that peace operations entail some uniform skills and duties across missions. Yet national militaries already have specialized units for particular tasks, and certain peacekeeping specializations would be extensions of these arrangements. Peace operations already rely extensively on civilian police units to maintain law and order, so specialization already exists to some degree.

Taking on new missions may also lead to changes in the agencies that organize peace operations. Rather than the Security Council of the UN or equivalent bodies in regional organizations authorizing and directing peace operations, perhaps some specialized agencies, such as the World Bank or the UN Department of Humanitarian Affairs, might become providers. The World Bank already has a unit on civil wars, so it is not inconceivable that the institution would expand further in its scope. It might also make some operational sense for such agencies to run their own peacebuilding operations. Better planning, coordination in the field, and longer-term commitments might result.

Sovereignty
During the Cold War, before a peacekeeping operation could be deployed, the state upon whose territory the peacekeepers would be deployed had to agree to the operation. In the post-Cold War era, peace operations were deployed in conflicts in which host-state cooperation was complete as well as when it was absent (and at several points in between). Such changes reflect a transformation in international norms vis-à-vis state sovereignty. The traditional notion was that sovereignty was almost absolute, what happened inside state borders being solely the domain of national governments. More recently, exceptions to state sovereignty have been carved out, most notably in the event of humanitarian disasters and widespread human rights violations (Weiss 2012). Sovereignty can be breached in the name of the responsibility to protect (R2P), as discussed in chapter 2. Accordingly, peace operations have been sent to areas without the full cooperation of the legally sovereign state (e.g., KFOR in Kosovo) or where no functioning government existed (UNOSOM I in Somalia).

The pendulum has not swung wholly in a direction oppo-
site that of state sovereignty, and there is considerable debate
as to exactly where the international community stands on the
limits of domestic jurisdiction. It is also the case that there
may be regional differences in conceptions of state sovereignty; Asian states (especially China) and African countries
have been resistant to new international forays into formerly
domestic domains. NATO sent a peace enforcement operation
during the Libyan civil war (2011), invoking the responsibility
to protect. Nevertheless, Syria, a much bloodier civil war, has
not received similar attention from the international community from its onset in 2011, at least through most of 2013.
Where will the line be drawn? Will the international community be willing and able to deploy peace operations in response
to any internal matters? Will such interventions be restricted
to internal matters that have significant negative externalities
(e.g., refugees, cross-border fighting)? Could peacekeepers
avoid cases in which there is disagreement over the need for
R2P between the major Security Council powers, or which
could turn into costly interventions over long periods of time?
Or, most unlikely, will the international community return to
more traditional notions of state sovereignty?

Peace operations will necessarily have to deal with whatever conception of sovereignty is adopted. This has important
implications for the range of possible missions that might be
assigned such operations. A looser conception of sovereignty
would expand the menu of options for peace operations,
enhancing some peacebuilding operations and extending
some missions to include human rights, economic development, and a series of other governmental functions. A stricter
constructionist view of sovereignty would make peace operations more reliant on host-state consent and probably restrict
missions to those closer to traditional peacekeeping and away
from peacebuilding, especially if the host state or host-state

area (in the case of failed states) is not supportive of such efforts. To the extent that state sovereignty erodes further, peacekeepers may be asked increasingly to take on active and primary (as opposed to third-party) roles in conflicts. In such cases, the ability of diplomatic efforts to resolve conflicts may give way to relying on peace operations to impose settlements through military force. This increases the risk to soldiers and may lead to an abandonment of impartiality as a central tenet of most peace operations.

The international community could develop its own guidelines for when peace operations might intervene. In some regions, such as the Western hemisphere, this may involve operations in support of democracy, a prevailing norm in the region. In other areas, the range of missions may be much narrower. Changing notions of sovereignty may empower multinational groupings to intervene in various conflicts, with operations more toward the coercive end of the continuum.

The international community also needs to decide if it wants to continue with the current liberal peacebuilding approach. A looser conception of sovereignty allows the peacekeepers to impose democracy and liberal economic policies in war-torn countries, as discussed in chapter 2. Although many criticisms of this liberal peacebuilding approach are ideologically driven, the peacekeepers face serious challenges that need to be addressed, including (a) limited understanding of domestic institutions, political culture, and local values in the processes of democratization and marketization, (b) tensions between military and civilian components, and (c) tensions between state-building and 'local ownership' goals. Yet the alternatives to liberal peacebuilding are often unattractive. One option is to do nothing and let the wars burn out, possibly resulting in hundreds of thousands of deaths, regional instability, and regional humanitarian crises. Another is to create trusteeships that are reminders of colonialism. A third is to accept undemocratically elected strongmen who could stabilize the conflict, but at the cost of democracy. None of the suggested alternatives to liberal peacekeeping is viable, and, while there are issues to be addressed within liberal peacebuilding, there is as yet no better approach.

It is also conceivable that the international community may choose to work more closely with host states. This would certainly smooth such operations in many ways. Yet there may be long delays in authorizing such missions as agents negotiate with local authorities. It was only after years of pressure and negotiation that the Sudanese government agreed to accept a joint UN–AU force, while thousands died in Darfur. Even then, host governments may place significant restrictions on peace operations such that mission success is jeopardized. The same Sudanese government announced in July 2007 that it would not permit any peace operation to have the right to use military force in an offensive fashion (robust peacekeeping), crippling the soldiers' ability to restrain armed militias. Ultimately, this may pose a "human rights dilemma" (Eide et al. 2005) for peacekeeping agents, as they must work with those who have poor human rights records to fulfill some mission tasks while retaining their role of outside critics of such abuses.

Sovereignty challenges extend beyond those concerned with host-state consent for certain activities. The actions of the peacekeepers and associated actors might affect the long-term autonomy and effectiveness of the host state. Barnett and Zurcher (2009) argue that some peacebuilding efforts actually reinforce weak states, as "contracts" between the peacebuilding operation and some local elites undermine structural reform; the self-interests of such elites may be best served by keeping the state weak in the long term. In other instances, peacebuilding is carried out largely by external actors, often dominated by the United States and Europe, and, in the process, agency is removed from the local population and institutions (Jabri 2010). There is a tension between doing what needs to be done in the short term and empowering indigenous actors to determine their own fates in the long term.

Political

Carrying Capacity
No form of governance (be it international, regional, or national) can provide unlimited services based on unlimited resources. That is, each governance structure has a "carrying capacity," or a maximum limit on how many services can be provided. The international community is similarly constrained with respect to conducting peace operations. Financial, political, and diplomatic resources are limited; or, at least, member states impose limits on how many operations can be conducted at any one time. The capacity of the international community for peace operations has expanded greatly in the 1990s and into the twenty-first century, with other agencies beyond the UN assuming some of the burden and states showing a greater willingness to support operations. At the end of 2012, there were fifty-three ongoing peace operations, a historical high. Nevertheless, greater demand for operations with the environmental challenges noted above may be on the horizon. Furthermore, the emphasis on more peacebuilding missions may place additional strains on organizational capacity, as these missions are larger and more expensive, and in theory will take longer to achieve success.

The obvious implications are that peace operations will, in the aggregate, require more resources and political attention in the future. The EU may have the resources to extend its participation in peace operations, but the AU does not. Africa is the site of more civil conflict than other continents, and the

AU already relies on support from other global and regional organizations to carry out its missions; any expansion of AU operations will require the UN, the EU, or individual states to come to its aid.

The major risks involved when the international community exceeds its carrying capacity in conducting peace operations are twofold. First, some peace operations that should have been authorized will not be, given the burden of existing operations. Which operations are selected and which are rejected may bear little relationship to security needs, but rather be driven instead by the scope of current commitments. Second, if the number of new operations is not stifled, newly authorized missions may be suboptimal in terms of their mandates, starting times, or resources (e.g., number of soldiers). Rather than there being individual instances of missed opportunities, all peace operations may be affected, as the burden of over-commitment is shared across operations.

The most obvious response to this challenge is to increase capacity or to come up with a better system of choosing where to place scarce resources. In terms of capacity expansion, there is little indication that the world community will infuse peace operations with permanent funding or troops, much less at the levels necessary to respond to all emergencies. More likely is a form of "triage" different from that described for the first challenge. Rather than selecting conflicts with the greatest chance of success, the UN and regional organizations may decide to focus (a) on conflicts with the greatest need or (b) on those that require the least resource commitment. The former is certainly defensible, in that the greatest threats receive the most attention, although it does mean that some conflicts are left to fester. The latter makes sense from a bureaucratic standpoint, but it is very short-sighted in terms of fulfilling broader global goals.

Limited carrying capacity might also precipitate some

organizational modifications and shifts. As implied above, the UN cannot systematically dump responsibility for some peace operations on regional organizations; many will need funding and logistical support from UN members anyway. Rather, there may need to be more hybrid operations with variable divisions of labor (funding from one source, troop provision from another, supplemental planning from a third) on cost-effectiveness grounds.

Greater use of private contractors has proven to be more cost-efficient and could be expanded for some tasks. Yet this creates another dilemma. Private contractors might raise the professionalism level of personnel, especially compared with soldiers from poor countries. The former might also fill in gaps left by organization members unwilling or unable to sustain commitments. Yet, in some cases, private contractors have undermined peacebuilding efforts by empowering indigenous subgroups whose interests do not necessarily match those of the country as a whole (Avant 2009). In addition, private contractors might lack the political and legal accountability for misdeeds that can be found with personnel from international organizations or national military units. Technology, such as passive monitoring mechanisms and satellites, might substitute for troops on the ground in carrying out traditional missions such as observing ceasefires and troop withdrawals. Yet, use of these technologies has political implications (Diehl 2002) that make them less than foolproof, including lacking the symbolic presence that UN soldiers have in deterring attacks. The UN and regional organizations might also delegate some peace operation responsibilities to selected individual states, essentially providing legitimizing authority but no other support to national military actions. This shifts the burden onto states, many of which have the capacity to carry out missions. The problem is finding states willing to take on such duties in areas or conflicts in which they have little interest. When such states do have interests and are willing to lead a peace operation unilaterally, there is the risk that national interests will trump international ones if states such as the United States, France, and the United Kingdom intervene.

Staying In vs. Getting Out
The UN (and this may be equally applicable to regional organizations as well) can be compared to a rude dinner guest who leaves early. Carrying capacity will influence when (if at all) peace operations are deployed; but, equally important, agents must find a balance between staying the course to finish a mission and getting out so that the state or territory in question can be self-governing. There are significant political pressures for member states of international organizations and multinational coalitions to leave prematurely, as arguably was the case with the withdrawal of UNSOM II forces from Somalia. Ongoing operational costs and deployment of troops in harm's way create such domestic political pressures. Also, diplomatic attention is devoted to peace operations early in their deployment, but such attention fades over time as new problems arise on international and regional policy agendas. Peacebuilding is a long-term process, but peace operations have actually become shorter in recent decades, even as their missions have become more multifaceted. At the other extreme, peace operations can become permanent in another sense – they are deployed for so long that they become an inherent part of the political situation in the area (e.g., UNIFIL, UNFICYP) rather than a temporary or transitional presence.

Premature withdrawal may have some disastrous consequences, not the least of which is the reversion to armed conflict. If peacebuilding operations are truncated, the process may be undermined and the state may reexperience instability.

That multiple peace operations have been deployed consecu-
tively to the same states (e.g., Haiti, Angola) suggests that the
first operations did not achieve their goals or the troops left
too early, before the missions were complete. In retrospect,
the international community may also have left East Timor
too soon, even though it appeared at the time that the newly
independent state was stable and economically viable. On the
other hand, as indicated in chapter 4, the presence of a peace
operation may actually inhibit conflict resolution and thereby
prolong the deployment of some operations even further. In
this way, some operations, especially traditional peacekeeping
ones, may prevent some long-term goals from being achieved.

How does the international community find a middle
ground between "peacekeeping fatigue" and being trapped in
long-term deployments? The obvious solution of strict time-
tables is actually not viable. First, setting a time limit at the
outset of operations is not necessarily realistic, even for missions such as election supervision that allegedly have a fixed
point or key event for termination. The processes of conflict
management and resolution are sometimes unpredictable,
and, while they are politically appealing, deadlines are often
not practical in reality. As indicated previously, the practice
of authorizing peace operations for six-month segments has
resulted only in repeated extensions of the missions. The
effect of setting a deadline and actually following it may result
in more premature withdrawals rather than fewer. At the
other end of the spectrum, it may be unrealistic to withdraw
forces from hotspots even if they have been deployed for many
years. The international community may find it desirable, but
too risky, to terminate an operation if the prospects of renewed
fighting as a result are great.

Options for dealing with this political challenge would seem
to fall on the domestic political and diplomatic fronts. The
creation of the UN Peacebuilding Commission, thereby involv-

ing key state actors in the deployment, strategy, and financing of decisions, is a first step. Greater rotation of soldiers and contributors would spread the burden of peace operations and make the missions less vulnerable to the withdrawal of continuing support by one or two key states. This is obviously easier in an organization with a large and diverse membership such as the UN than it is in small regional organizations. Multinational coalitions may need to be enlarged at their outset or mid-course to be sustained. Diplomatic efforts by the sponsoring agencies could also be enhanced so that progress is more likely in management and resolution. Such progress is likely to sustain operations, as members will be more inclined to pull out when the prospects for ultimate success are distant and uncertain. Similarly, renewed diplomatic efforts may lead to final resolutions of conflict, so that, when they do withdraw, peace operations can do so confident that the local environment is stable and likely to remain so in the long run.

Even if the problem of premature withdrawal is solved, there remains the accompanying dilemma that staying too long can have deleterious effects on the local society. Edelstein (2009) refers to the "duration dilemma," in which foreign forces might be essential to maintain security and deter renewed fighting but their continuing presence is increasingly resented by the local population, who are impatient with progress and desire a greater role in their own peacebuilding. He also refers to the "footprint dilemma," which refers largely to the size of the peacebuilding force. Too small an operation and it might not be big enough to be effective in its mission. Too many peacekeepers and attendant personnel, and the operation might dominate the local governing structures and become more vulnerable to the duration dilemma. As is clear from these dilemmas and the risk of early withdrawal that it is difficult to find a balance in terms of timing and force for the operation.

Capacity

The Need for Coordination

In their infancy, traditional peacekeeping operations were relatively uncomplicated. The UN was largely responsible for securing commitments from contributing states, and the actual conduct of the operation was left to a commander and national military units. Planning procedures were limited, and monitoring of operations was very crudely done through the 1980s. As peacekeeping missions expanded, the inadequacy of these arrangements became apparent. In large part, this was the impetus behind the Brahimi Report and its reforms. This represented progress, albeit still incomplete, in the planning and conduct of peace operations, but in many ways the changes proposed responded better to the problems of the past than the challenges of the future. The Brahimi reforms were also confined to the United Nations, whereas now approximately half of operations are conducted by other agents. The Peacebuilding Commission reflects the need for coordination, but that organization is only advisory, and it is supported by a relatively small staff in the Peacebuilding Support Office. Furthermore, the Peacebuilding Commission has not filled what had been referred to as the "gaping hole" in coordination (Paris 2009). It could play a greater role, however, in ensuring that contribution promises are fulfilled, create units such as one on the rule of law that offer coordination possibilities with other UN units, and generally be given more authority for planning and coordination activities (Bellamy 2010).

Peace operation agents will face enormous coordination problems in the future, and to some extent already do. This is partly a function of the number of different actors involved, directly and indirectly, in these missions. There are more than a dozen different regional organizations that have sent at least one peace operation, in addition to the peace operations of the United Nations and those that are multinational in character. The majority of peace operations are deployed in conflicts in which the missions of other institutions are already present. Within peacebuilding efforts, the military aspect must be coordinated with the economic, social, political, and humanitarian efforts that are occurring. This may involve other units of the organizing agent (e.g., the UN Department of Humanitarian Affairs), other international organizations (e.g., the World Bank or regional development banks), NGOs (e.g., Doctors without Borders), and, potentially, other private entities. This is in addition to coordinating with local actors, groups, militias, and government officials. Hybrid operations may add to the complexity, as different tasks are assigned or shared among other agents.

Lack of effective coordination will undermine the efficiency of operations, especially multidimensional peacebuilding operations. It may also limit the effectiveness of those operations in the long run. Paris (2004) has noted that, unless there is effective economic growth and the development of proper electoral systems, a renewal of violence and the collapse of operations may result. Thus, failure in one part of an operation may have spillover effects on the other missions, and a "security first" strategy may prove to be short-sighted. Good management also requires accountability for actions, and thereby the development of adaptive policies. Ineffective coordination muddles who is responsible for different elements of the operation and makes mid-course adjustments difficult when needed.

One dilemma is that coordination goes beyond merely bringing together multiple actors. International organization agencies, governments, NGOs, and other actors are not simply different organizationally; they also may have fundamental philosophical differences that can hinder cooperation

(Paris 2009). Government elites have vested interests in sustaining their power and influence within states, whereas NGOs have bureaucratic interests in retaining control over resources and ensuring long-term influence in the country. International organizations, and the leading states that guide them, are prone to support Western, liberal models of development and state-building that clash with the interests and approaches of other actors. The net effect is that the various actors might favor competing goals and strategies, and each retains some incentives not to work with the others.

As each mission is to some degree unique, it is probably not possible or advisable to develop one model of coordination. Indeed, a leading study group warned against fixed templates in favor of the "form should follow function" principle (Eide et al. 2005). Still, agreements between peace operation agents, states, and/or other organizations might be a first step in laying out the framework for cooperation. Because peace operations are developed on an ad hoc basis and often need to be deployed quickly, such agreements cannot be negotiated on the spot. Yet a broad delineation of tasks and responsibilities can be achieved ahead of time and executed as needed.

Balas (2011b) suggests that the model of the EU Cell at NATO's strategic command, SHAPE, should be implemented by all major international organizations that contribute to peace operations. At the bare minimum, these organizations should have liaison officers for peace operations at each other's headquarters. Another suggestion for increased cooperation would be to transform the bilateral summits between two international organizations (e.g., the UN and the EU) into multilateral summits between all major agencies sending peace operations. Yearly multilateral summits on peace operations between the different international organizations active in this field would allow for better coordination and cooperation, both at the headquarters and in the field. In addition, the

UN, regional organizations, and NGOs could develop some common standards (standards exist for each of these sets of actors, but they are not always congruent with one another) for the conduct of such operations. Within the United Nations system, cooperation between the DPKO, the Department of Political Affairs, the UN Development Programme, and other agencies responsible for conflict management and development is channeled through the Executive Committee on Peace and Security. In the field, however, the two communities (conflict management and development) operate separately, but "staff secondments and provision of space, services, and logistical support are not uncommon" (Griffin 2003: 208). A good example of this is the quick impact project, a relatively recent addition to the tasks of peace operations, in which peacekeepers cooperate with NGOs to address the development needs of local communities (building a well/medical clinic, repairing a road/bridge, etc.). This peacekeeping–humanitarian/ development cooperation could be institutionalized. Thus, for example, the delivery of humanitarian assistance could follow select protocols, with different actors responsible for various tasks and coordination rules and task sequencing specified. In addition, integrated missions could develop a series of other protocols for coordination, including a joint operations center, policy planning capacities, and real-time evaluation mechanisms.[1]

Readiness for Robust Peacekeeping
The failure of collective security systems in the League of Nations and the United Nations left the international community with no capacity for actions requiring significant military capacity and high levels of coercion. To some extent, this gap was filled by regional military alliances, such as NATO. Traditional peacekeeping operations were designed to be almost the antithesis of military operations, and, accordingly,

the lack of coercive capacity was not an issue; no missions required it, and indeed coercive force would have undermined the purposes and goals of the peacekeeping mission.

As peace operations have evolved, however, they have been asked to take on missions that occur in a context of active fighting (e.g., during the second phase of conflict); these include actions such as pacification, delivering humanitarian assistance under hostile conditions, and restraining wrong-doing such as genocide. The rules of engagement for these missions allow a greater use of offensive military force – and a greater military capacity is certainly needed for mission success. For example, MINUSMA, an operation authorized in 2013 for deployment to Mali, requires such a capacity to carry out its stabilization mission. Yet most peace operations still lack the capacity, in terms of planning and configuration, for robust peacekeeping. This goes beyond the ad hoc arrangements of how the force is constituted to cover how the force is equipped and what kinds of action are allowed by its mandate. Perhaps only NATO (and to a lesser extent the EU) among international forces has the necessary ability to take coercive military action.

The lack of an effective coercive capacity among global organizations has two pernicious effects. First, it may mean that organizations pass on peace operations that they should have undertaken. Increasingly, the international community faces humanitarian and other disasters in the midst of civil wars. To ignore or underserve such needs means greater loss of life and perhaps more dire outcomes (e.g., failed states, increased refugee flows) later – problems even more difficult with which the international community and peace operations ultimately have to deal. Second, if peace operations are deployed to address such problems, they may be ill-equipped to complete their missions successfully. UN forces in Bosnia (UNPROFOR) were weak, unable to deliver humanitarian assistance in corridors controlled by Serb forces, and almost helpless to stop the bombing of civilians in Srebrenica. In particular, coercive military action may be essential to preempt or defeat spoilers as well as to protect civilian populations.

As noted in chapter 3, proposals for a permanent peace or rapid deployment force have generally not reached fruition, and their prospects are at best uncertain in the near future. Moreover, such plans address the needs for speed and efficiency more than for enhanced military capacity. More realistic is that the world will rely on states with significant military power to carry out such operations. This could be in the form of those states participating in operations conducted by the UN or regional organizations. More likely, regional or global powers (e.g., the United States, France, the United Kingdom, Australia, Russia, Nigeria, and South Africa) will lead unilateral or multinational peace efforts. International organizations may pass resolutions legitimizing such actions, but the states involved would have full control over the direction of the operations. This introduces a particularly vexing dilemma. On the one hand, it solves much of the capacity problem, as such national militaries are well equipped to carry out coercive missions. On the other hand, essentially subcontracting such activities to national governments creates other difficulties. The resulting operations are not necessarily accountable to regional and global community interests, as it is presumed that the leading states will protect their own interests first, and these may or may not correspond to those of the broader international community. The long-term involvement of these states in unstable areas, or the imposition of settlements by such states, runs the risk of operations becoming imperialistic and undermining rights of national self-determination and autonomy.

Training

In the early days of peace operations, training issues arose because traditional peacekeeping missions were different than standard military ones (see chapter 1 for a comparison). Complicating this now is the expansion of new missions associated with peacebuilding, many of which involve skills different from even traditional peacekeeping. As the global community increases the number and type of peace operations, it must give more attention to the preparedness of its soldiers, and this has several dimensions.

Most soldiers receive extensive military training in basic combat skills. These may be fine for some peace operation activities on the coercive end of the scale. Yet other missions depend for their effectiveness on a complex set of what has been referred to as "contact" (more diplomatic) skills. For example, missions whose primary purpose is monitoring call for observational and analytical skills. Those that attempt to restore countries to functioning civil societies require a much broader range of skills, including interpersonal and intergroup relations, communication, negotiation, and, in the case of military operations, a mix of combat and political skills. Organizational skills are needed for missions intended to limit damage, such as humanitarian assistance, or to rebuild institutions, infrastructure, and local economies, such as development assistance. A key question, however, is whether soldiers are actually being trained in contact skills. A survey of peacekeeping training programs (reported in Diehl, Druckman, and Wall 1998) noted that few emphasize these competencies. Given the increased frequency with which such skills are used in current missions, it is apparent that a significant gap exists between training and practice.

A second set of concerns is the compatibility of the training that peacekeepers might receive for the different types of missions. One issue is whether a given soldier can master all the techniques and behaviors outlined above, assuming that present or expanded training regimens could accommodate them. Will training in one approach undermine the training required in another approach? A further concern is with the ability of soldiers to shift orientations and techniques as the mission evolves. Related to these issues is whether it is advisable to separate missions closer to traditional peacekeeping from those carried out for more traditional military purposes.

Traditional war fighting will continue to be a mission for most national militaries, one that will necessarily be a top priority. Will soldiers' war-fighting skills be compromised? For example, traditional peacekeeping operations usually entail rules of engagement that permit a soldier to fire a weapon only in self-defense, something that is counter to conventional military strategy and, indeed, many newer peace missions. There is also tremendous variation in training and professionalism across national militaries, making peace operations subject to problems associated with the least common denominator of preparedness.

Peace operations won't be effective at a micro-level and may jeopardize some macro-goals if the soldiers don't have the proper skills necessary to carry out the mission. For example, the lack of appropriate negotiation skills at a roadblock inspection of vehicles could damage relations and cooperation with the local population; it might also undermine trust in the operation among other conflict actors who rely on peacekeepers to detect weapons smuggling. Although the overall mission may not be jeopardized, mistakes by peacekeepers may result in civilian deaths or make the peacekeepers themselves vulnerable to violent action.

There has been an improvement in training regimens for peacekeepers over the last decade such that most national militaries no longer insist that the standard military training is all that is needed for peace operation duty. Some states,

such as the Nordic countries, have conducted joint peacekeeping training for years, and private organizations such as the
International Peace Institute have sponsored workshops and
seminars on peace operation practice. Still, with the complexity
of peace missions increasing, there are several other potential
responses rather than simply relying on existing programs or
their expansion. One is the establishment of common training regimens for UN and regional organizations; states would
not be permitted to participate in peace operations without
meeting certain standards. This would raise the level of professionalism, promote standard practices, and ensure some
minimum level of competence. Yet such a requirement may
discourage troop contributions, something more tolerable
in a context of excess troop supply than one in which securing troop contributions is problematic, as in the status quo.
It may also be necessary for the international community to
adopt a peace operation specialty within national militaries,
admittedly a luxury for some poor countries. Peacekeeping
soldiers would receive specialized training for peace operations only and not be assigned to traditional military units. In
some ways, this would be the equivalent of earmarking troops
for peace operations, but involving a less formal commitment
than the proposals described in chapter 3. This plan might
even make states willing to contribute forces to peace operations if they already have units dedicated to such missions. Yet
most national militaries would have to overcome their own
cultures, which treat peace operations as secondary missions
– a career as a peacekeeper being regarded as less prestigious
than that involved in traditional war fighting. The dramatic
expansion in the use of civilian police in peace operations is
indicative of another approach. Specialized personnel outside
conventional military establishments might be called upon to
perform certain specialized duties.

A training-related dilemma is the apparent discrepancy

between the high civilian personnel vacancy rates for some peace operations, especially in Africa (on average 22 percent, but for some cases twice as high; for more information, see de Coning 2010), and the availability of large numbers of trained peacekeeping personnel. A study by Solli, de Carvalho, de Coning, and Pedersen (2011) argues that there are large numbers of civilian personnel attending peacekeeping training, but many of these individuals are never deployed to the field. Solli and his colleagues point to a number of structural bottlenecks having to do mostly with the DPKO/Department of Field Support recruitment system and the use of personnel referrals to get to work in a peace operation. Training centers should work closer with the recruitment offices of international organizations in order to allow peace operations to take advantage of skilled personnel and deploy as many peacekeepers as authorized. Avoiding situations in which less than 60 percent of the peacekeepers authorized were actually deployed a year after the start of the operation (e.g., UNAMID in Darfur) will most likely have an impact on the success of the intervention, too.

Overarching Challenges

Unintended Consequences and Interactions with the Local Population
The purposes of peace operations are multifaceted, including preventing the renewal of violence as well as a number of other goals specific to the mandate of a given operation. As noted above, these provide the bases for evaluating the success or failure of the operation. Yet peace operations also have a number of other outcomes, many of which are unintended and undesirable.[2] These unintended consequences come in a variety of forms. Some are gender-based, as peacekeeping soldiers commit rapes against the local population, spread

HIV/AIDS, and may perpetuate discriminatory hiring practices when employing the local population.[3] For example, in 2007, UN peacekeepers (in the UNOCI mission in Côte d'Ivoire) were accused of rape and sexual abuse, the latest in a string of similar allegations against peacekeeping personnel around the world (see Nordas and Rustad 2013 for when such abuses are more likely).

Economic distortions may occur from the presence of peace operations, especially peacebuilding ones. These include the creation of dual public-sector economies (that of the peacebuilding operation and that of the national government) and the undermining of local markets for services and products because of the displacement of the same by the peace operation. Political corruption, black market activity, and other effects are also possible; these might be committed by peacekeepers or facilitated by their presence (Andreas 2008).

Such outcomes leave many new victims of conflict, but, unlike those killed or displaced by war, these are the direct result of peace operation actions and clearly avoidable. Furthermore, the negative economic and political consequences undermine the long-term goals of stability and economic growth that are prerequisites to the maintenance of peace and security in the area.

Peace operations face several dilemmas in promoting economic development in post-conflict situations. On the one hand, peacebuilding efforts to stabilize and stimulate the economy are based on Western models of liberalism, and this has some value in preparing states to be part of the global economy. On the other hand, this model has been criticized as one that removes autonomy from local actors (Jabri 2010) and creates institutions and processes that are incompatible with local culture. Those efforts are directed too much toward external markets and actors, without enough attention being paid to local reconstruction (Williams 2010).

A second dilemma arises when peace operations and attendant peacebuilding efforts supply massive amounts of economic and humanitarian aid to the host country. Such aid might be essential to stabilize the state and to save lives, especially when the aid is in the form of food and medical supplies. Yet too much aid and for too long a period creates a dependent relationship between the host state and international donors (Narten 2009). Failure to promote local ownership of problems and solutions does not permit the local population and its leaders to make progress and ultimately move away from external influence.

The UN has not been blind to all these problems, although it is not clear that comparable scrutiny has been given to them by regional organizations and multinational coalitions. The UN has established a Conduct and Discipline Unit and tested an anti-prostitution unit in its Kosovo operation. Thanks to the work of these new units, and after the adoption of a UN General Assembly resolution (A/RES/57/306) asking for "zero tolerance" on sexual exploitation and abuse, in 2012 there were sixty allegations of sexual exploitation and abuse committed by UN peacekeepers, a significant reduction from the 367 allegations reported in 2006. But almost half of the sixty allegations involved the most egregious forms of sexual exploitation and abuse: sexual activity with minors and rape.

While the sexual abuse incidents have garnered substantial media attention, issues of economic dislocation and corruption are more pervasive but less identifiable by single incidents; accordingly, there has been less scrutiny and action on these problems. A first step might be incorporating the possibility of such effects into peace operation planning. Although they may be unintended consequences, they need not be unanticipated ones, and therefore policymakers may be able to eliminate or mitigate these effects by redesign or counter-action. Understanding the local context and the potential negative consequences of peace operations for the local society, assessing the needs of the local population (see Pouligny 2006), and providing solutions such as quick impact projects to some of their immediate needs may alleviate some of the problems. Better monitoring and the holding of those responsible for violations may also lead to an improvement in the situation. For transgressions of individual soldiers, it becomes the responsibility of national militaries to take action, regardless of the agent organizing the mission. Yet if the national militaries refuse even to investigate the allegations, the agent organizing the mission should conduct the investigation.

The Lack of Political Will

The most frequent explanation for the failure of peace operations is that the international community "lacked the political will" to act or acted without sufficient vigor and commitment to make the operation a success. Yet too often this is fallacious, as it begs the question; that is, the lack of political will is inferred from the failure of the peace operation and the assumption that the failure was because the international community did not do enough – otherwise it would have been successful. Still, one should not abandon the lack of political will explanation completely, but instead ask what it was that the international community was unwilling to do, and why.

When it is stated that the UN or a regional organization lacked the political will to act, it is really the member states that bear responsibility, not the organizational bureaucracies or their leaderships. The so-called lack of political will is manifested in numerous ways. Member states may not be reluctant to act but merely disagree on what actions to take. Decisions to launch peace operations by international organizations are collective decisions, and the failure to act may be the result of irreconcilable differences on what the proper course of action should be. Depending on the rules of the organization, one state opposing action or holding different views from others may be sufficient to block action. For example, there was considerable disagreement in the UN over how to intervene in Darfur, with China leading the opposition to coercive intervention. It may also be the case that, when peace operations are authorized, the mandate reflects the least common denominator of agreement among the member states, and the resulting peace operation (e.g., UNAMIR in Rwanda) is inadequate to the task. Thus, one should not confuse the lack of political will with disagreements within the authorizing agencies.

Nevertheless, there are instances in which there is consensus among member states not to act or to act only in a limited fashion when responding to international crises. Such may be an unwillingness to grant too much power or autonomy to the sponsoring organization. It may also reflect a reluctance of a state to set a precedent (e.g., a coercive peace operation that protects human rights) that could lead to intervention against itself or its allies in the future. Lack of political will may also, in truth, be an unwillingness to bear the personnel or financial burdens associated with new operations. Finally, lack of political will may actually be a realpolitik calculation that a peace operation, or at least one with sufficient mandate and power, does not serve the national interests of certain member states, especially those that are the most powerful in the organization. If peace operations were strongly in the interests of key states, we might expect many more unilateral or small multinational efforts when deadlocks emerge in the UN or regional organizations. This is not the case, as much of the demand for peace operations, especially in the post-Cold War era, has been in Africa and elsewhere at the periphery of major or regional power interests.

Unpacking the "lack of political will" reveals a multitude of motivations for states to block or limit peace operations. There is no policy or solution that can magically alter the international political system and its operating rules. What is required is a normative change in which international interests supersede those of individual states. This is not necessarily a Pollyannaish dream. Over the last centuries, the international community has made great strides in constructing human rights norms, developing environmental standards, and taking other steps to promote the collective good, even at the expense of national interest. At the same time, there has been movement toward granting greater autonomy and responsibility to international organizations, especially in Europe, for certain tasks. None of these changes occurred quickly, and one might expect that peace operations for the foreseeable future will be subject to what will be labeled the lack of political will; but the growth in the number and scope of peace operations indicates that such will is greater than it has ever been, even as it is not as strong as it might be.

Appendix: Peace Operations, 1948–2012

Acronym	Full mission name	Host country	Start date	End date
UNGOMAP, OSGAP	UN Good Offices Mission in Afghanistan and Pakistan, Office of the Secretary-General for Afghanistan and Pakistan	Afghanistan	1988	1989
ISAF	NATO International Security Assistance Force	Afghanistan	2001	
UNAMA	UN Assistance Mission in Afghanistan	Afghanistan	2002	
EUPOL	EU Police Mission in Afghanistan	Afghanistan	2007	
MPF–Operation Alba	Multinational Peace Force "Operation Alba"	Albania	1997	1997
OSCE Presence in Albania	OSCE Presence in Albania	Albania	1997	
AFOR	NATO Albanian Force	Albania	1999	1999
UNAVEM I	UN Angola Verification Mission I	Angola	1989	1991
UNAVEM II	UN Angola Verification Mission II	Angola	1991	1995
UNAVEM III	UN Angola Verification Mission III	Angola	1995	1997
MONUA	UN Observer Mission in Angola	Angola	1997	1999
UNPROFOR–BH	UN Protection Force Bosnia and Herzegovina	Bosnia	1992	1995
RRF	NATO Rapid Reaction Force	Bosnia	1995	1995
IFOR	NATO Implementation Force	Bosnia	1995	1996
UNMIBH	UN Mission in Bosnia and Herzegovina	Bosnia	1995	2002
OSCE Mission to Bosnia and Herzegovina	OSCE Mission to Bosnia and Herzegovina	Bosnia	1995	
SFOR	NATO Stabilization Force	Bosnia	1996	2004
EUPM	EU Police Mission in Bosnia and Herzegovina	Bosnia	2003	2012
EUFOR Althea	European Union Military Operation in Bosnia and Herzegovina	Bosnia	2004	
OMIB	OAU Observer Mission in Burundi	Burundi	1994	1996
AMIB	African Mission in Burundi	Burundi	2003	2004
ONUB	UN Operation in Burundi	Burundi	2004	2006
BINUB	UN Integrated Office in Burundi	Burundi	2006	
AU STF	AU Special Task Force	Burundi	2007	2010
UNAMIC	UN Advance Mission in Cambodia	Cambodia	1991	1992

Acronym	Full mission name	Host country	Start date	End date
UNTAC	UN Transitional Authority in Cambodia	Cambodia	1992	1993
MISAB	Inter-African Force to Monitor the Implementation of the Bangui Agreements	Central African Republic (CAR)	1997	1998
MINURCA	UN Mission in the Central African Republic	CAR	1998	2000
FOMUC	CEMAC Multinational Force in Central Africa	CAR	2002	2008
MINURCAT	UN Mission in the Central African Republic and Chad	CAR	2007	2010
EUFOR Chad–CAR	EU Military Bridging Operation in Chad and the CAR	CAR	2008	2009
MICOPAX I	ECCAS Mission for the Consolidation of Peace	CAR	2008	
ONUCA	UN Observer Group in Central America	Central America	1989	1992
Chad I	Chad I	Chad	1979	1979
Chad II	Chad II	Chad	1980	1980
Chad III	Chad III	Chad	1981	1982
UNASOG	UN Aouzou Strip Observer Group	Chad, Libya	1994	1994
OAS/MAPP	OAS Mission to Support the Peace Process in Colombia	Colombia	2004	
OMIC	OAU Observer Mission in the Comoros	Comoros	1997	1999
ONUC	UN Operation in the Congo	Democratic Republic (DR) of Congo	1960	1964
SADC Operation Sovereign Legitimacy	SADC Operation Sovereign Legitimacy	DR Congo	1998	2003
OAU Observer Mission	OAU Observer Mission	DR Congo	1999	2000
MONUC	UN Organization Mission in the Democratic Republic of the Congo	DR Congo	1999	2010
Operation Artemis	EU Military Operation in the Democratic Republic of the Congo	DR Congo	2003	2003
EUSEC	EU Advisory and Assistance Mission for Security Reform in the Democratic Republic of Congo	DR Congo	2005	
EUPOL Congo	EU Police Mission in the Democratic Republic of Congo	DR Congo	2007	
MONUSCO	UN Organization Stabilization Mission in the Democratic Republic of the Congo	DR Congo	2010	
OAS Mil Experts Comm	OAS Committee of Military Experts	Costa Rica, Nicaragua	1955	1955
ECOMICI	Economic Community of West African States Mission in Côte d'Ivoire	Côte d'Ivoire	2003	2004
MINUCI	UN Mission in Côte d'Ivoire	Côte d'Ivoire	2003	2004
Operation Licorne	Operation Licorne	Côte d'Ivoire	2003	

Acronym	Full mission name	Host country	Start date	End date
UNOCI	UN Operation in Côte d'Ivoire	Côte d'Ivoire	2004	
UNPROFOR–C, UNCRO	UN Protection Force – Croatia, UN Confidence Restoration Operation	Croatia	1992	1995
UNPF	UN Peace Force	Croatia	1996	1996
UNTAES	UN Transitional Administration for Eastern Slavonia, Baranja, and Western Sirmium	Croatia	1996	1998
UNMOP	UN Mission of Observers in Prevlaka	Croatia	1996	2002
OSCE Mission to Croatia	OSCE Mission – Croatia	Croatia	1998	2000
UNFICYP	UN Peacekeeping Force in Cyprus	Cyprus	1964	
OAS IAPF	OAS Inter-American Peace Force	Dominican Republic	1965	1966
MFO	Multinational Force and Observers	Egypt (Sinai)	1982	
ONUSAL	UN Observer Mission in El Salvador	El Salvador	1991	1995
OSCE Mission to Estonia	OSCE Mission to Estonia	Estonia	1992	2001
UNMEE	UN Mission in Ethiopia and Eritrea	Ethiopia, Eritrea	2000	2008
OLMEE	AU Liaison Mission in Ethiopia–Eritrea	Ethiopia, Eritrea	2000	2008
So. Ossetia Jnt Force	South Ossetia Joint Force	Georgia	1992	
Russian Abkhazia Peacekeeping Operation	Russian Abkhazia Peacekeeping Operation	Georgia	1993	1994
UNOMIG	UN Observer Mission in Georgia	Georgia	1993	2009
OSCE Mission to Georgia	OSCE Mission to Georgia	Georgia	1994	2008
CPKF/CPFOR	CIS Collective Peacekeeping Force in Georgia/Collective Peacemaking Force	Georgia	1994	
EUJUST Themis	EU Rule of Law Mission in Georgia	Georgia	2004	2005
EUMM	EU Monitoring Mission in Georgia	Georgia	2008	
MINUGUA	UN Verification Mission in Guatemala	Guatemala	1997	1997
ECOMOG	Economic Community of West African States Monitoring – Guinea Bissau	Guinea-Bissau	1998	1999
UNIOGBIS	UN Integrated Peacebuilding Office in Guinea-Bissau	Guinea-Bissau	1999	
EU SSR Guinea-Bissau	EU Mission in Support of Security Sector Reform in Guinea-Bissau	Guinea-Bissau	2008	2010
UNMIH	UN Mission in Haiti	Haiti	1993	1996
MICIVIH	International Civilian Mission in Haiti	Haiti	1993	1999
Operation Uphold Democracy	Operation Uphold Democracy	Haiti	1994	1995
UNSMIH	UN Support Mission in Haiti	Haiti	1996	1997
UNTMIH	UN Transition Mission in Haiti	Haiti	1997	1997
MIPONUH	UN Civilian Police Mission in Haiti	Haiti	1997	2000

Acronym	Full mission name	Host country	Start date	End date
MIFH	Multinational Interim Force in Haiti	Haiti	2004	2004
MINUSTAH	UN Stabilization Mission in Haiti	Haiti	2004	
OAS Mil Obsvrs II	OAS Military Observers II	Honduras, El Salvador	1976	1981
OAS CMOG	OAS Civil–Military Operation Group	Honduras, Nicaragua	1957	1957
UNMOGIP	UN Military Observer Group in India and Pakistan	India, Pakistan	1949	
UNIPOM	UN India–Pakistan Observation Mission	India, Pakistan	1965	1966
Aceh Monitoring Mission	EU Monitoring Mission in Aceh	Indonesia (Aceh)	2005	2006
UNIIMOG	UN Iran–Iraq Military Observer Group	Iran, Iraq	1988	1991
OIF, res 1483	Operation Iraqi Freedom	Iraq	2003	2003
UNAMI	UN Assistance Mission for Iraq	Iraq	2003	
NATO's Training in Iraq	NATO's Training in Iraq	Iraq	2004	2011
EUJUST LEX	EU Integrated Rule of Law Mission for Iraq	Iraq	2005	
UNEF I	First UN Emergency Force	Israel, Egypt	1956	1967
UNEF II	Second UN Emergency Force	Israel, Egypt	1973	1979
UNTSO	UN Truce Supervision Organization	Israel, Egypt, Lebanon, Syria	1948	
UNDOF	UN Disengagement Observer Force	Israel, Syria	1974	
EUBAM Rafah	EU Border Assistance Mission for the Rafah Crossing Point	Israel/Palestine	2005	
EUPOL COPPS	EU Coordinating Office for Palestinian Police Support	Israel/Palestine	2006	
OSCE Mission to Kosovo, Sandjak and Vojvodina	OSCE Mission to Kosovo, Sandjak and Vojvodina	Kosovo	1992	1993
OSCE Verification Mission to Kosovo	OSCE Verification Mission to Kosovo	Kosovo	1999	1999
KFOR	NATO Kosovo Force	Kosovo	1999	
OSCE Mission in Kosovo	OSCE Mission in Kosovo	Kosovo	1999	
UNMIK	UN Interim Administration Mission in Kosovo	Kosovo	1999	
EULEX Kosovo	EU Rule of Law Mission in Kosovo	Kosovo	2008	
LAS	Arab League Security Force in Kuwait	Kuwait	1961	1963
UNIKOM	UN Iraq–Kuwait Observation Mission	Kuwait, Iraq	1991	2003
OSCE Mission to Latvia	OSCE Mission to Latvia	Latvia	1993	2001
UNOGIL	UN Observation Group in Lebanon	Lebanon	1958	1958
ADF	League of Arab States Arab Deterrent Force	Lebanon	1976	1982
UNIFIL	UN Interim Force in Lebanon	Lebanon	1978	

Acronym	Full mission name	Host country	Start date	End date
MNF I	Multinational Force I	Lebanon	1982	1982
MNF II	Multinational Force II	Lebanon	1982	1984
SADC	SADC Operation Boleas	Lesotho	1998	1999
ECOMOG	Economic Community of West African States Monitoring Group–Liberia	Liberia	1990	1999
UNOMIL	UN Observer Mission in Liberia	Liberia	1993	1997
ECOMIL	Economic Community of West African States Mission in Liberia	Liberia	2003	2003
UNMIL	UN Mission in Liberia	Liberia	2003	
NATO Libya	NATO Operation Unified Protector	Libya	2011	2011
UNSMIL	UN Support Mission in Libya	Libya	2011	
OSCE Skopje Spill-Over	OSCE Skopje Spill-Over	Former Yugoslav Republic (FYR) of Macedonia	1992	
UNPREDEP	UN Preventive Deployment Force	FYR Macedonia	1993	1999
KFOR	NATO Kosovo Force	FYR Macedonia	1999	
Essential Harvest	NATO Operation Essential Harvest	FYR Macedonia	2001	2001
Amber Fox	NATO Operation Amber Fox	FYR Macedonia	2001	2002
Allied Harmony	NATO Operation Allied Harmony	FYR Macedonia	2002	2003
EUFOR Concordia	EU Military Operation in the FYR of Macedonia	FYR Macedonia	2003	2003
EUPOL Proxima	EU Police Mission in the FYR of Macedonia	FYR Macedonia	2003	2005
EUPAT	EU Police Advisory Team in the FYR of Macedonia	FYR Macedonia	2005	2006
EUTM Mali	EU Training Mission in Mali	Mali	2013	
MINUSMA	Multidimensional Integrated Stabilization Mission in Mali	Mali	2013	
Moldova Joint Force/Joint Control Commission PK Force	Moldova Joint Force/Joint Control Commission PK Force	Moldova	1992	
OSCE Mission to Moldova	OSCE Mission to Moldova	Moldova	1993	
EUBAM	EU Border Assistance Mission to Moldova and Ukraine	Moldova	2005	
ONUMOZ	UN Operation in Mozambique	Mozambique	1992	1994
UNTAG	UN Transition Assistance Group	Namibia	1989	1990
UNMIN	UN Mission in Nepal	Nepal	2007	2011
CIAV–OAS	International Support and Verification Commission – OAS	Nicaragua	1989	1997
EUCAP Sahel Niger	EU Capacity Building Sahel Niger	Niger	2012	

Acronym	Full mission name	Host country	Start date	End date
TMG	Bougainville Truce Monitoring Group	Papua New Guinea (Bougainville)	1997	1998
PMG	Bougainville Peace Monitoring Group	Papua New Guinea (Bougainville)	1998	2003
MOMEP	Mission of Military Observers Ecuador–Peru	Peru, Ecuador	1995	1999
OSCE Mission to Chechnya	OSCE Mission to Chechnya	Russia (Chechnya)	1995	2003
OAU NMOG I	OAU Neutral Military Observer Group I	Rwanda	1991	1992
OAU NMOG II	OAU Neutral Military Observer Group II	Rwanda	1992	1993
UNAMIR I	UN Assistance Mission for Rwanda	Rwanda	1993	1994
Operation Turquoise	Operation Turquoise	Rwanda	1994	1994
UNAMIR II	UN Assistance Mission for Rwanda II	Rwanda	1994	1996
UNOMUR	UN Observer Mission Uganda–Rwanda	Rwanda, Uganda	1993	1994
ECOMOG	Economic Community of West African States Monitoring Group–Sierra Leone	Sierra Leone	1997	2000
UNOMSIL	UN Observer Mission in Sierra Leone	Sierra Leone	1998	1999
UNAMSIL	UN Mission in Sierra Leone	Sierra Leone	1999	2005
UNIOSIL	UN Integrated Office in Sierra Leone	Sierra Leone	2006	2008
UNIPSIL	UN Integrated Peacebuilding Office in Sierra Leone	Sierra Leone	2008	
CMPAG	Commonwealth Multinational Police Assistance Group	Solomon Islands	2000	2000
IPMT	International Peace Monitoring Team for the Solomon Islands	Solomon Islands	2000	2002
RAMSI	Pacific Islands Forum Regional Assistance Mission to the Solomon Islands	Solomon Islands	2003	
UNITAF	Unified Task Force	Somalia	1992	1993
UNOSOM I	UN Operation in Somalia I	Somalia	1992	1993
UNOSOM II	UN Operation in Somalia II	Somalia	1993	1995
AMISOM	African Union Mission in Somalia	Somalia	2007	
NATO	NATO Operation Ocean Shield	Somalia	2007	
EU NAVFOR	EU Naval Force Somalia	Somalia	2008	
EUTM Somalia	EU Somalia Training Mission	Somalia	2010	
EUCAP Nestor	EU Regional Maritime Capacity Building for the Horn of Africa and the Western Indian Ocean	Somalia	2012	
UNMISS	UN Mission in the Republic of South Sudan	South Sudan	2011	
IPKF	Indian Peacekeeping Force	Sri Lanka	1987	1990
AMIS	African Mission in Sudan	Sudan	2004	2007
EU–AMIS	EU Support to AMIS	Sudan	2005	2007
UNMIS	UN Mission in the Sudan	Sudan	2005	2011

Acronym	Full mission name	Host country	Start date	End date
UNAMID	United Nations–African Union Mission in Darfur	Sudan	2007	
UNISFA	UN Interim Security Force for Abyei	Sudan/South Sudan	2011	
OAS	OAS Special Mission to Suriname	Suriname	1992	2000
UNSMIS	UN Supervision Mission in Syria	Syria	2012	2012
CPKF	CIS Collective Peacekeeping Forces/CIS Tajikistan Buffer Force	Tajikistan	1993	2000
UNMOT	UN Mission of Observers in Tajikistan	Tajikistan	1994	2000
OSCE Mission to Tajikistan	OSCE Mission to Tajikistan	Tajikistan	1994	2002
INTERFET	International Force for East Timor	Timor-Leste	1999	2000
UNTAET	UN Transitional Administration in East Timor	Timor-Leste	1999	2002
UNMISET	UN Mission of Support in East Timor	Timor-Leste	2002	2005
UNOTIL	UN Office in Timor-Leste	Timor-Leste	2005	2006
UNMIT	UN Integrated Mission in Timor-Leste	Timor-Leste	2006	2012
OSCE Mission to Ukraine	OSCE Mission to Ukraine	Ukraine	1994	1999
UNTEA/UNSF	UN Temporary Executive Authority in West New Guinea/UN Security Force in West New Guinea	West New Guinea	1962	1963
MINURSO	UN Mission for the Referendum in Western Sahara	Western Sahara	1991	
UNYOM	UN Yemen Observation Mission	Yemen	1963	1964
CMF	Commonwealth Monitoring Force	Zimbabwe	1979	1980

Source: Balas (2011b).

Notes

1 We will use the term "peace operation" rather than the colloquial "peacekeeping" throughout this book to refer to such operations. We do, however, refer to the soldiers in peace operations as "peacekeepers" regardless of mission.
2 Quoted in Hoyng and Koelbl (2007).
3 The first edition of this book was published in 1992, but we cite its replacement – the more recent, revised edition that appeared in 1995.
4 See also Talentino (2004) and Barnett et al. (2007).
5 See also Paris (2004).
6 Technically, the optimal collective security system is one that never needs to be operational. Potential aggressors would be deterred by the prospect of other states coming to the aid of potential victims. The impossibility of defeating united forces against them would be sufficient to deter any aggressive action.

CHAPTER 2 THE HISTORICAL EVOLUTION AND RECORD OF PEACE OPERATIONS

1 The sections on the early history are adapted and abridged from Diehl (1994, pp. 1–32), © the Johns Hopkins University Press, reprinted with permission of the Johns Hopkins University Press. Sections on the development of peacebuilding are adapted and abridged from Diehl (2006), repr. with permission of Thomson Publishing.
2 See also Goodrich (1957).

3 For a full history of League of Nations actions, see Northedge (1986).
4 For more details, see James (1994).
5 See Malone and Wermester (2000); Paris (2004); Talentino (2004).
6 In scholarly terms, this means that there are "selection effects." Peace operations are "selected" into a non-random sample of conflicts, and this has implications for how we might assess their success, both theoretically and methodologically. For example, if peace operations are sent primarily to intractable conflicts, it will not be surprising if a disproportionate number fail.
7 For a critique of this position, see Jakobsen (1996) and Andersson (2000).
8 The length is measured in years, with any fraction of a calendar year counted as a full year. The mean actually underestimates the true average, given that many of the operations are ongoing, and therefore the data are "right-censored," with most of those operations likely to continue beyond 2013.
9 For these analyses, purely military operations and counter-insurgency operations, such as the US invasion of Iraq, were dropped.

CHAPTER 3 THE ORGANIZATION OF PEACE OPERATIONS

1 The *Report of the panel on United Nations peace operations*, released in 2000, is available at www.unrol.org/files/brahimi%20report% 20peacekeeping.pdf.
2 The Commission is a subsidiary advisory organ of both the General Assembly and the Security Council.
3 For an overview of contemporary regional peace operations, see Bellamy and Williams (2005).
4 There is also some variation within these organizations, and, accordingly, we use the EU operation in Bosnia (EUFOR) and the AU mission in Sudan (AMIS) as examples.
5 UNAMET was the small mission of the United Nations, three months long, that was tasked with organizing the referendum on independence.
6 The death toll in Darfur since 2003 is subject to some debate, but

most estimate the minimum to be in the hundreds of thousands, and more than 2 million people have been displaced.

7 See Salerno et al. (2000) and Sullivan and Cohen (2000); for the political implications, see Diehl (2002).

8 See Boehmer, Gartzke, and Nordstrom (2004).

9 China and Brazil deploy their peacekeepers only through the United Nations, while South Africa uses regional organizations, the SADC and AU, in addition to the UN.

10 A full discussion of this topic is given in Pichat (2004).

11 Commission on Global Governance (1995); Henderson (1995); Boutros-Ghali (1995); D'Orville and Najman (1995); Ford Foundation (1993); Mendez (1997).

CHAPTER 5 TEN CHALLENGES FOR FUTURE PEACE OPERATIONS

1 For a full analysis of the problems of integrated missions and a host of recommended solutions, see Eide et al. (2005).

2 For a full discussion of all the unintended consequences, see the individual chapters in Aoi, de Conging, and Thakur (2007).

3 For the sources of some of these problems, see Higate (2007).

References and Suggested Readings

Aksu, E. (2003) *The United Nations, intra-state peacekeeping and normative change.* New York: Manchester University Press.

Andersson, A. (2000) "Democracies and UN peacekeeping operations, 1990–1996," *International Peacekeeping*, 7, pp. 1–22.

Andreas, P. (2008) *Blue Helmets and Black Markets.* Ithaca, NY: Cornell University Press.

Aoi, C., de Conging, C., and Thakur, R. (2007) *Unintended consequences of peacekeeping operations.* Hong Kong: United Nations University Press.

Autesserre, S. (2010) *The trouble with the Congo: Local violence and the failure of international peacebuilding.* Cambridge: Cambridge University Press.

Avant, D. (2009) "Making peacemakers out of spoilers: International organizations, private military training, and statebuilding after war," in R. Paris and T. D. Sisk (eds), *The dilemmas of statebuilding: Confronting the contradictions of postwar peace operations.* London: Routledge, pp. 104–26.

Balas, A. (2011a) "It takes two (or more) to keep the peace: Multiple simultaneous peace operations," *Journal of International Peacekeeping*, 15, pp. 384–421.

Balas, A. (2011b) "Creating global synergies: Inter-organizational cooperation in peace operations," unpublished doctoral dissertation, University of Illinois at Urbana-Champaign.

Balas, A., Owsiak, A., and Diehl, P. F. (2012) "Demanding peace: The impact of prevailing conflict on the shift from peacekeeping to peacebuilding," *Peace & Change*, 37, pp. 195–226.

Barnett, M., and Zurcher, C. (2009) "The peacebuilder's contract: How external statebuilding reinforces weak statehood," in R. Paris and T. D. Sisk (eds), *The dilemmas of statebuilding: Confronting the contradictions of postwar peace operations.* London: Routledge, pp. 23–52.

Barnett, M., Kim, H., O'Donnell, M., and Sitea, L. (2007) "Peacebuilding: What is in a name?," *Global Governance*, 13, pp. 35–58.

Beardsley, K. (2011) "Peacekeeping and the contagion of armed conflict," *Journal of Politics*, 73, pp. 1051–64.

Bellamy, A. J. (2010) "The institutionalisation of peacebuilding: What role for the UN Peacebuilding Commission?," in O. P. Richmond (ed.), *Peacebuilding: Critical developments and approaches*. London: Palgrave Macmillan, pp. 193–212.

Bellamy, A. J., and Williams, P. (2004) "Conclusion: What future for peace operations? Brahimi and beyond," *International Peacekeeping*, 11, pp. 183–212.

Bellamy, A. J., and Williams, P. (2005) "Who's keeping the peace? Regionalization and contemporary peace operations," *International Security*, 29, pp. 157–95.

Bellamy, A. J., and Williams, P. (2012) "Local politics and international partnerships: The UN Operation in Côte d'Ivoire (UNOCI)," *Journal of International Peacekeeping*, 16, pp. 252–81.

Bellamy, A. J., Williams, P., and Griffin, S. (2010) *Understanding peacekeeping*. 2nd edn, Cambridge: Polity.

Benner, T., Mergenthaler, S., and Rotmann, P. (2011) *The new world of UN peace operations: Learning to build peace*. Oxford: Oxford University Press.

Berdal, M., and Economides, S. (eds) (2007) *United Nations intervention 1991–2004*. Cambridge: Cambridge University Press.

Boehmer, C., Gartzke, E., and Nordstrom, T. (2004) "Do intergovernmental organizations promote peace?", *World Politics*, 57, pp. 1–38.

Boulden, J. (2001) *Peace enforcement: The United Nations experience in Congo, Somalia, and Bosnia*. Hartford, CT: Praeger.

Boutros-Ghali, B. (1995) *An agenda for peace*. 2nd edn, New York: United Nations.

Boyd, J. (1971) *United Nations peacekeeping operations*. New York: Praeger.

Brahimi, L. (2000) *Report of the panel on United Nations peace operations*, www.unrol.org/files/brahimi%20report%20peacekeeping. pdf (accessed September 19, 2013).

Bratt, D. (1996) "Assessing the success of UN peacekeeping operations," *International Peacekeeping*, 3, pp. 64–81.

Bratt, D. (1997) "Explaining peacekeeping performance: The UN in internal conflicts," *International Peacekeeping*, 4, pp. 45–70.

Bratt, D. (2002) "Blue condoms: The use of international

peacekeepers in the fight against AIDS," *International Peacekeeping*, 9, pp. 65–86.

Brooks, D. (2000) "Messiahs or mercenaries? The future of international private military services," *International Peacekeeping*, 4, pp. 129–44.

Brubaker, R. (1996) *Nationalism reframed: Nationhood and the national question in the new Europe*. Cambridge: Cambridge University Press.

Bueger, C., Stockbruegger, J., and Werthes, S. (2011) "Pirates, fishermen and peacebuilding: Options for counter-piracy strategy in Somalia," *Contemporary Security Policy*, 32, pp. 356–81.

Call, C., and Cousens, E. (2008) "Ending wars and building peace: International responses to war-torn societies," *International Studies Perspectives*, 9, pp. 1–21.

Caplan, R. (2005) *International governance of war-torn territories: Rule and reconstruction*. New York: Oxford University Press.

Cassidy, R. M. (2004) *Peacekeeping in the abyss: British and American peacekeeping doctrine and practice after the Cold War*. Hartford, CT: Praeger.

Center on International Cooperation (2012) *Annual review of global peace operations, 2012*. Boulder, CO: Lynne Rienner.

Claude, I. (1971) *Swords into plowshares: The problems and progress of international organization*. 4th edn, New York: Random House.

Cockell, J. (2000) "Conceptualizing peacebuilding: Human security and sustainable peace," in M. Pugh (ed.), *Regeneration of war-torn societies*. London: Macmillan, pp. 15–34.

Collier, P., Hoeffler, A., and Soderbom, M. (2006) *Post conflict risks*, CSAE WPS/2006-12, August 17. University of Oxford, Center for the Study of African Economies.

Commission on Global Governance (1995) *Our global neighbourhood*. Oxford: Oxford University Press.

Cousens, E. (2001) "Introduction," in E. Cousens and C. Kumar, with K. Wermester (eds), *Peacebuilding as politics: Cultivating peace in fragile societies*. Boulder, CO: Lynne Rienner, pp. 1–20.

Daudelin, J., and Seymour, L. (2002) "Peace operations finance and the political economy of a way out," *International Peacekeeping*, 8, pp. 99–117.

de Coning, C. H. (2010) *Civilian capacity in United Nations peacekeeping and peacebuilding missions*, Policy Brief no. 4. Oslo: Norwegian Institute for International Affairs (NUPI).

de Oliveira, G. C. (2012) "Naval peacekeeping and piracy: Time for a critical turn in the debate," *International Peacekeeping*, 19, pp. 48–61.

Derblom, M., Frisell, E. H., and Schmidt, J. (2008) *UN–EU–AU coordination in peace operations in Africa*. Stockholm: Swedish Defense Research Agency.

Diehl, P. F. (1994) *International peacekeeping*. Rev. edn, Baltimore: Johns Hopkins University Press.

Diehl, P. F. (2000) "Forks in the road: Theoretical and policy concerns for 21st century peacekeeping," *Global Society*, 14, pp. 337–60.

Diehl, P. F. (2002) "The political implications of using new technologies in peace operations," *International Peacekeeping*, 9, pp. 1–24.

Diehl, P. F. (2006) "Paths to peacebuilding: The transformation of peace operations," in T. D. Mason and J. D. Meernik (eds), *Conflict prevention and peacebuilding in post-war societies: Sustaining the peace*. New York: Routledge, pp. 107–29.

Diehl, P. F., and Druckman, D. (2010) *Evaluating peace operations*. Boulder, CO: Lynne Rienner.

Diehl, P. F., Druckman, D., and Wall, J. (1998) "International peacekeeping and conflict resolution: A taxonomic analysis with implications," *Journal of Conflict Resolution*, 42, pp. 33–55.

D'Orville, H., and Najman, D. (1995) "A new system to finance the United Nations," *Futures*, 27, pp. 171–9.

Doyle, M., and Sambanis, N. (2000) "International peacebuilding: A theoretical and quantitative analysis," *American Political Science Review*, 94, pp. 779–802.

Doyle, M., and Sambanis, N. (2006) *Making war and building peace: United Nations peace operations*. Princeton, NJ: Princeton University Press.

Druckman, D., and Stern, P. C. (1997) "The forum: Evaluating peacekeeping missions," *Mershon International Studies Review*, 41, pp. 151–65.

Edelstein, D. M. (2009) "Foreign militaries, sustainable institutions, and postwar statebuilding," in R. Paris and T. D. Sisk (eds), *The dilemmas of statebuilding: Confronting the contradictions of postwar peace operations*. London: Routledge, pp. 81–103.

Eide, E., Kaspersen, A., Kent, R., and von Hippel, K. (2005) *Report on integrated missions: Practical perspectives and recommendations*. New York: United Nations Office for the Coordination of Humanitarian Affairs (OCHA).

European Union (2007) *Treaty of Lisbon amending the Treaty on European*

Union and the Treaty Establishing the European Community, 2007/C 306/01, December 13, www.unhcr.org/refworld/docid/476258d32. html (accessed March 7, 2013).

Fearon, J. (1995) "Rationalist explanations for war," International Organization, 49, pp. 379–414.

Fetherston, A. B. (1994) Towards a theory of United Nations peacekeeping. New York: St Martin's Press.

Ford Foundation (1993) Financing an effective United Nations: A report of the independent advisory group on UN financing. New York: Ford Foundation.

Fortna, V. P. (2003) "Inside and out: peacekeeping and the duration of peace after civil and interstate wars," International Studies Review, 5, pp. 97–114.

Fortna, V. P. (2004a) "Does peacekeeping keep peace? International intervention and the duration of peace after civil war," International Studies Quarterly, 48, pp. 269–92.

Fortna, V. P. (2004b) "Interstate peacekeeping: Causal mechanism and empirical effects," World Politics, 56, pp. 481–519.

Fortna, V. P. (2008) Does peacekeeping work?. Princeton, NJ: Princeton University Press.

Gäfvert, B. (1995) "Swedish troops in international cooperation – North Africa, 1802 and Fyn-Schleswig 1848–1850," in Lars Ericson (ed.), Solidarity and defence: Sweden's armed forces in international peace-keeping operations during the 19th and 20th centuries. Stockholm: Swedish Military History Commission, pp. 23–33.

Gibbs, D. (1997) "Is peacekeeping a new form of imperialism?," International Peacekeeping, 4, pp. 122–8.

Gill, B., and Huang, C. (2009) China's expanding role in peacekeeping: Prospects and Policy Implications, Policy Paper no. 25. Stockholm: SIPRI.

Gilligan, M., and Stedman, S. (2003) "Where do the peacekeepers go?," International Studies Review, 5/4, pp. 37–54.

Goetz, A. M. (2008) "Introduction," presented at the conference "Women Targeted or Affected by Armed Conflict: What Role for Military Peacekeepers?," Wilton Park, Sussex, May 27–29, www.unifem.org/attachments/events/WiltonParkConference_ Presentations_200805.pdf (accessed March 7, 2013).

Goodrich, L. (1957) "Efforts to establish international police force down to 1950," in W. Frye (ed.), A United Nations peace force. New York: Oceana, pp. 172–94.

Goulding, M. (1993) "The evolution of United Nations peacekeeping," *International Affairs*, 69, pp. 451–64.

Green, D. M., Kahl, C. H., and Diehl, P. F. (1998a) "Predicting the size of UN peacekeeping operations," *Armed Forces & Society*, 24, pp. 485–500.

Green, D. M., Kahl, C. H., and Diehl, P. F. (1998b) "The price of peace: A predictive model of UN peacekeeping fiscal costs," *Policy Studies Journal*, 26, pp. 620–35.

Greig, M., and Diehl, P. F. (2005) "The peacekeeping–peacemaking dilemma," *International Studies Quarterly*, 49, pp. 621–45.

Griffin, M. (2003) "The helmet and the hoe: Linkages between United Nations development assistance and conflict management," *Global Governance*, 9, pp. 199–217.

Guéhenno, J.-M. (2006) "UN embraces 'robust peacekeeping' including the use of force: A conversation with Jean-Marie Guehenno," *European Affairs*, Spring–Summer, pp. 14–25.

Gurr, T. R., Woodward, M., and Marshall, M. (2005) "Forecasting instability: Are ethnic wars and Muslim countries different?," paper presented at the annual meeting of the American Political Science Association, Washington, DC, September 1–5.

Hansen, A. (2002) *From Congo to Kosovo: Civilian police in peace operations*, Adelphi Paper 343. London: International Institute for Strategic Studies and Oxford University Press.

Hartz, H. (1999) "CIVPOL: The UN instrument for police reform," *International Peacekeeping*, 6, pp. 27–42.

Heldt, B. (2001) "Conditions for successful intrastate peacekeeping missions," paper presented at Euroconference, San Feliu de Guixols, Spain, October 6–11.

Henderson, H. (1995) "New markets and new commons: Opportunities in the global casino," *Futures*, 27, pp. 113–24.

Hewitt, J. J. (2008) "Trends in global conflict, 1946–2005," in J. J. Hewitt, J. Wilkenfeld, and T. R. Gurr (eds), *Peace and conflict 2008*. Boulder, CO: Paradigm, pp. 21–6.

Hewitt, J. J., Wilkenfeld, J., and Gurr, T. R. (2008) *Peace and Conflict 2008*. Boulder, CO: Paradigm.

Higate, P. (2007) "Peacekeepers, masculinities, and sexual exploitation," *Men and Masculinities*, 10, pp. 99–119.

Holt, V., Taylor, G., and Kelly, M. (2009) *Protecting civilians in the context of UN peacekeeping operations: Successes, setbacks and remaining challenges*. New York: United Nations.

Hoyng, H., and Koelbl, S. (2007) "Peacekeeping is a very ambiguous term", Spiegel Online, www.spiegel.de/international/world/spiegel-interview-with-nato-commander-john-craddock-peacekeeping-is-a-very-ambiguous-term-a-481740.html (accessed October 10, 2013).

Howard, L. M. (2008) *UN peacekeeping in civil wars*. Cambridge: Cambridge University Press.

Human Security Report Project (2012) *Human Security Report 2012*, www.hsrgroup.org/human-security-reports/2012/overview.aspx (accessed March 10, 2013).

IPI (International Peace Institute) (2013) *Strengthening the UN Peacebuilding Commission*, www.ipinst.org/publication/meeting-notes/detail/393-strengthening-the-un-peacebuilding-commission.html (accessed March 10, 2013).

Jabri, V. (2010) "War, government, politics: A critical response to the hegemony of the liberal peace," in O. P Richmond (ed.), *Peacebuilding: Critical developments and approaches*. London: Palgrave Macmillan, pp. 41–57.

Jakobsen, P. V. (1996) "National interest, humanitarianism or CNN: What triggers UN peace enforcement after the Cold War?," *Journal of Peace Research*, 33, pp. 205–15.

Jakobsen, P. V. (2002) "The transformation of United Nations peace operations in the 1990s: Adding globalization to the conventional 'end of the Cold War explanation,'" *Cooperation and Conflict*, 37, pp. 267–82.

James, A. (1990) *Peacekeeping in international politics*. London: Macillan.

James, A. (1994) "Internal peacekeeping," in D. A. Charters (ed.), *Peacekeeping and the challenge of civil conflict resolution*. Center for Conflict Studies, University of New Brunswick, pp. 44–58.

Jenkins, R. (2013) *Peacebuilding: From concept to commission*. London: Routledge.

Jett, D. C. (2000) *Why peacekeeping fails*. New York: St Martin's Press.

Lawyer, J. F. (2005) "Military effectiveness and economic efficiency in peacekeeping: Public versus private," *Oxford Development Studies*, 33, pp. 99–106.

Lindsay, D. (2007) *Promoting peace with information: Transparency as a tool of security*. Princeton, NJ: Princeton University Press.

Mackinlay, J. (1990) "Powerful peace-keepers," *Survival*, 32, pp. 241–50.

Mackinlay, J., and Chopra, J. (1992) "Second generation multinational operations," *Washington Quarterly*, 15, pp. 113–31.

Maley, W., Sampford, C., and Thakur, R. (2003) *From civil strife to civil society: Civil and military responsibilities in disrupted states*. New York: United Nations University Press.

Malone, D., and Wermester, K. (2000) "Boom or bust? The changing nature of UN peacekeeping," *International Peacekeeping*, 7, pp. 37–54.

Manning, C. (2003) "Local level challenges to post-conflict peacebuilding," *International Peacekeeping*, 10, pp. 25–43.

Mansfield, E., and Snyder, J. (2005) *Electing to fight: Why emerging democracies go to war*. Cambridge, MA: MIT Press.

Martin-Brule, S.-M. (2012) "Assessing peace operations' mitigated outcomes," *International Peacekeeping*, 19, pp. 235–50.

McQueen, N. (2002) *United Nations peacekeeping in Africa since 1960*. London: Pearson Education.

Mendez, R. (1997) "Financing the United Nations and the international public sector: Problems and reform," *Global Governance*, 3, pp. 283–310.

Mullenbach, M. J. (2005) "Deciding to keep peace: An analysis of international influences on the establishment of third-party peacekeeping missions," *International Studies Quarterly*, 49, pp. 529–56.

Narten, J. (2009) "Dilemmas of promoting 'local ownership': The case of Kosovo," in R. Paris and T. D. Sisk (eds), *The dilemmas of statebuilding: Confronting the contradictions of postwar peace operations*. London: Routledge, pp. 252–84.

Neack, L. (1995) "UN peace-keeping: In the interest of community or self?," *Journal of Peace Research*, 32, pp. 181–96.

Newman, E., and Schnabel, A. (eds) (2002) "Recovering from civil conflict: Reconciliation, peace, and development," special issue of *International Peacekeeping*, 9.

Nitzschke, H., and Studdard, K. (2005) "The legacies of war economies: Challenges and options for peacekeeping and peacebuilding," *International Peacekeeping*, 12, pp. 222–39.

Nordas, R., and Rustad, S. (2013) "Sexual exploitation and abuse by peacekeepers: Understanding variation," *International Interactions*, 39, pp. 511–34.

Northedge, F. S. (1986) *The League of Nations: Its life and times, 1920–1946*. New York: Holmes & Meier.

Norton, A. R. (1991) "The demise of the MN," in A. McDermott and K. Skjelsbaek (eds), *The multinational force in Beirut, 1982–1984*. Miami: Florida International University Press, pp. 80–94.

Oudraat, C. de J. (1996) "The United Nations and internal conflict," in M. Brown (ed.), *International dimensions of internal conflicts.* Cambridge, MA: MIT Press.

Paris, R. (1997) "Peacebuilding and the limits of liberal internationalism," *International Security,* 22, pp. 54–89.

Paris, R. (2004) *At war's end: Building peace after civil conflict.* Cambridge: Cambridge University Press.

Paris, R. (2009) "Understanding the 'coordination problem' in postwar statebuilding," in R. Paris and T. D. Sisk (eds), *The dilemmas of statebuilding: Confronting the contradictions of postwar peace operations.* London: Routledge, pp. 53–78.

Paris, R. (2010) "Saving liberal peacebuilding," *Review of International Studies,* 36, pp. 337–65.

Paris, R., and Sisk, T. D. (eds) (2009) *The dilemmas of statebuilding: Confronting the contradictions of postwar peace operations.* London: Routledge.

Pichat, S. K. (2004) *A UN "legion": Between utopia and reality.* New York: Frank Cass.

Pouligny, B. (2006) *Peace operations seen from below: UN missions and local people.* London: Hurst.

Pugh, M. (2000) "Introduction: The ownership of regeneration and peacebuilding," in M. Pugh (ed.), *Regeneration of war-torn societies.* London: Macmillan, pp. 1–12.

Pushkina, D. (2006) "A recipe for success? Ingredients of a successful peacekeeping mission," *International Peacekeeping,* 13, pp. 133–49.

Ramsbottom, O. (2000) "Reflections on UN post-settlement peacebuilding," *International Peacekeeping,* 7, pp. 167–89.

Ratner, S. (1995) *The new UN peacekeeping: Building peace in lands of conflict after the Cold War.* New York: St Martin's Press.

Richmond, O. P. (ed.) (2010) *Peacebuilding: Critical developments and approaches.* London: Palgrave Macmillan.

Rikhye, I. J. (1984) *The theory and practice of peacekeeping.* New York: St Martin's Press.

Russett, B. (1997) "Ten balances for weighing UN reform proposals," in B. Russett (ed.), *The once and future security council.* New York: St Martin's Press, pp. 13–28.

Salerno, R., Vannoni, M., Barber, D., Parish, R., and Frerichs, R. (2000) *Enhanced peacekeeping with monitoring technologies.* Albuquerque, NM: Sandia National Laboratories.

Sambanis, N. (1999) "The UN operation in Cyprus: A new look

at the peacekeeping–peacemaking relationship," *International Peacekeeping*, 6, pp. 79–108.

Schmidl, E. A. (2000) "The evolution of peace operations from the nineteenth century," in E. A. Schmidl (ed.), *Peace operations between peace and war*. London: Frank Cass, pp. 4–20.

Schnabel, A. (2002) "Post-conflict peacebuilding and second-generation preventive action," *International Peacekeeping*, 9, pp. 7–30.

Segal, D. (1995) "Five phases of United Nations peacekeeping: An evolutionary typology," *Journal of Political and Military Sociology*, 23, pp. 65–79.

Sisk, T. D. (2008) "Peacebuilding as democratization: Findings and recommendations," in A. Jarstad and T. Sisk (eds), *From war to democracy: Dilemmas of peacebuilding*. Cambridge: Cambridge University Press.

Skogmo, B. (1989) *UNIFIL: International peacekeeping in Lebanon, 1978–1988*. Boulder, CO: Lynne Rienner.

Solli, A., de Carvalho, B., de Coning, C., and Pedersen, M. F. (2011) "Training in vain? Bottlenecks in deploying civilians for UN peacekeeping," *International Peacekeeping*, 18, pp. 425–38.

Stedman, S., Rothchild, D., and Cousens, E. (2002) *Ending civil wars: The implementation of peace agreements*. Boulder, CO: Lynne Rienner.

Sullivan, J. D., and Cohen, S. P. (2000) *Technology for peace: Enhancing the effectiveness of multinational interventions*. Urbana, IL: United States Institute of Peace, Program in Arms Control, Disarmament, and International Security.

Talentino, A. (2004) "One step forward, one step back? The development of peacebuilding as concept and strategy," *Journal of Conflict Studies*, 25, pp. 33–60.

Tardy, T. (2006) "The EU and NATO as peacekeepers: Open cooperation versus implicit competition," in H. Ojanen (ed.), *Peacekeeping – peacebuilding: Preparing for the future*. Helsinki: Finnish Institute for International Affairs.

Thaker, R., and Schnabel, A. (2001) *United Nations peacekeeping operations: Ad hoc missions, permanent engagement*. New York: United Nations University Press.

Tobin, J. (1978) "A proposal for monetary reform," *Eastern Economic Journal*, 4, pp. 153–9.

United Nations (1999) *United Nations Security Council Resolution 1264*, S/RES/1264, September 15.

United Nations (2007) *The United Nations and Darfur*, fact sheet. New York: United Nations Department of Public Information.

United Nations (2008) *United Nations peacekeeping operations: Principles and guidelines*. New York: United Nations Department of Peacekeeping Operations, Best Practices Section.

United Nations (2009a) United Nations Security Council Resolution 1894, S/RES/1894, November 11.

United Nations (2009b) *A New Partnership Agenda: Charting a New Horizon for UN Peacekeeping*. New York: United Nations Department of Peacekeeping Operations and Department of Field Support.

United Nations (2010) *Status of contributions to the regular budget, international tribunals, peacekeeping operations and capital master plan*. New York: United Nations Department of Public Information.

United Nations (2012) *United Nations Peacekeeping Operations Factsheet: 31 December 2012*, www.un.org/en/peacekeeping/archive/2012/bnote1212.pdf (accessed September 19, 2013).

Urquhart, B. (1983) "Peacekeeping: a view from the operational center," in H. Wiseman (ed.), *Peacekeeping appraisals and proposals*. New York: Pergamon Press, pp. 161–74.

Wainhouse, D. (1966) *International peace observation*. Baltimore: Johns Hopkins University Press.

Wallensteen, P., and Heldt, B. (2008) "International peacekeeping: The UN versus regional organizations," in J. J. Hewitt, J. Wilkenfeld, and T. R. Gurr (eds), *Peace and conflict 2008*. Boulder, CO: Paradigm, pp. 93–106.

Weiss, T. G. (2012) *Humanitarian intervention: Ideas in action*. 2nd edn, Cambridge: Polity.

Wesley, M. (1997) *Casualties of the new world order: The causes of failure of UN missions to civil wars*. New York: St Martin's Press.

Wiharta, S., Melvin, N., and Avezov, X. (2012) *The new geopolitics of peace operations: Mapping the emerging landscape*. Stockholm: SIPRI.

Williams, A. J. (2010) "Reconstruction: The missing historical link," in O. P. Richmond (ed.), *Peacebuilding: Critical developments and approaches*. London: Palgrave Macmillan, pp. 58–73.

Wiseman, H. (1987) "United Nations peacekeeping: An historical overview," in H. Wiseman (ed.), *Peacekeeping: Appraisals and proposals*. New York: Pergamon Press, pp. 19–63.

Wood, E. J. (2003) "Civil wars: What we don't know," *Global Governance*, 9, pp. 247–60.

Wright, T., and Greig, J. M. (2012) "Staying the course: Assessing the durability of peacekeeping operations," *International Studies Quarterly*, 29, pp. 127–47.

Zartman, I. W. (2000) "Ripeness: The hurting stalemate and beyond," in P. Stern and D. Druckman (eds), *International conflict resolution after the Cold War*. Washington, DC: National Academic Press, pp. 225–50.

Index